CAMBRIDGE TEXTBOOKS IN LING

MW01039866

General Editors: B. COMRIE, C. J. FILLMORE,
J. LYONS, P. H. MATTHEWS, R. POSNER, S. Rⵖ ... ⵖ, ⵖ. ⵖ. SMITH,
N. VINCENT

TENSE

TENSE

BERNARD COMRIE

DEPARTMENT OF LINGUISTICS,
UNIVERSITY OF SOUTHERN CALIFORNIA

CAMBRIDGE
UNIVERSITY PRESS

CAMBRIDGE UNIVERSITY PRESS
Cambridge, New York, Melbourne, Madrid, Cape Town, Singapore, São Paulo

Cambridge University Press
The Edinburgh Building, Cambridge CB2 2RU, UK

Published in the United States of America by Cambridge University Press, New York

www.cambridge.org
Information on this title: www.cambridge.org/9780521236522

© Cambridge University Press 1985

First published 1985
Eighth printing 2004

A catalogue record for this publication is available from the British Library

Library of Congress Catalogue Card Number: 84–23832

ISBN-13 978-0-521-23652-2 hardback
ISBN-10 0-521-23652-5 hardback

ISBN-13 978-0-521-28138-6 paperback
ISBN-10 0-521-28138-5 paperback

Transferred to digital printing 2006

CONTENTS

Contents

PREFACE

My aim in writing this book has been to provide an introduction to the nature of tense in language. This has entailed two more specific objectives: first, the definition of tense (Chapter 1, especially section 1.4), and, secondly, an account of the range of variation found in tense systems across the languages of the world. Because of this second more specific aim, I have tried to make the book rich in illustrative material from a wide range of languages. However, it should always be borne in mind that this material is presented not solely as being of interest in its own right or to specialists in that particular language; rather, the language-specific material is designed to illustrate the range of variation found cross-linguistically and to suggest the limitations which a general theory of tense must place on such possibilities for variation.

It is my belief that the best pedagogical approach is to present a coherent account of some domain, rather than to attempt to describe in overview the full range of theories and pre-theoretical statements that have been made about that domain. I have not, therefore, felt myself obliged to take account of the various competing approaches to tense that abound in the general and language-specific literature. I have striven rather to present and justify the approach that I believe to be correct; in a few instances, where I am genuinely unsure as to the relative merits of competing viewpoints, I have indicated this. As discussed in chapter 1, I take tense to be defined as the grammaticalisation of location in time, and I believe that at least much of what has traditionally been called tense does fall under this definition. While I believe that this approach to tense is correct, clearly if the reader, having worked through the various data and claims presented in this book, can show that they can be accounted for more elegantly in a theory where tense is not viewed in this way, then I still believe that the presentation of a range of tense data in this book will have served a purpose in the advancement of our science.

Unlike much recent work on tense, the present book contains little by way of formalism, nor is it written within the framework of any specific current theory of linguistics. This is not intended as a denigration of work in these areas, in particular tense logic. Rather, I believe that there is a certain systematised set of facts about tense in human language that must be taken into account by any general theory of tense, and therefore by any general theory of language that incorporates an account of tense. It is these facts that I have attempted to systematise in the present work. I believe that this should serve as a corrective to current formal approaches to the representation of tense which do not take account of the range of variation found across languages, or conversely predict a greater range of variation than is possible in human language. It is therefore to be hoped that this book will lead to a dialogue between those interested in establishing the range of tense oppositions made cross-linguistically or in individual languages, and those interested in constructing a formal theory of tense or in incorporating such a formal approach into a formal theory of language overall. Some suggestions as to how the material in this book might serve to foster a more formal account are given in chapter 6.

The approach outlined in the previous paragraph is felt by many linguists to be un-theoretical (a-theoretical, even anti-theoretical). This is not my intention nor, I believe, my achievement. My aim in this book is to present a theory of tense, a theory which is sensitive both to the range of tense oppositions found cross-linguistically and to the limitations on that variation. My ultimate hope is, of course, that the ideas propounded in this book will be incorporated into a more general theory of language, but at the very least the ideas contained in this book will provide constraints on the evaluation of such a theory in terms of its adequacy in handling material on tense. When these ideas on tense are incorporated into a more general theory, then the more general theory may well suggest further questions about tense which have been overlooked in the present work. This is simply the general interaction between work in a specific sub-domain of linguistics and the overall theoretical framework. I would be sad indeed if the present book had exhausted all the interesting questions that could be asked about tense. On the other hand, my hope for the future is somewhat tempered by the fact that many current linguistic theories (as opposed to theories specifically about tense) seem to have remarkably little of interest to say about tense.

The main area of concentration of this book is the typology of tense, i.e. establishment of the range within which languages can vary in the grammaticalised expression of location in time. There are many adjacent areas which I have chosen not to discuss in this book, not because I feel that they are uninteresting, but because I am either not competent to discuss them and evaluate the often conflicting literature concerning them, or because they would take me too far afield from my main concerns. I have already mentioned tense logic, although I believe that a thorough grounding in tense logic will prove an invaluable aid in trying to integrate the ideas contained in this book into a more general formal theoretical perspective. In addition, I have not considered the acquisition of tense systems, whether by first or second language learners. I have not discussed in detail the use of tense in discourse: this decision is likely to be particularly controversial, and I have therefore included some justification for my position here in section 1.8. Finally, I have not considered in any detail recent work on the psychology, philosophy, or physics of time; the discussion of conceptualisation of time in section 1.2 is no doubt naive, but I believe justified by the kinds of time location distinctions found in natural language. While I find current philosophical work on the nature of time fascinating, it is not clear to me that it provides any insight into the linguistic phenomenon of tense.

Examples from languages other than English are usually presented as given in the source cited, or transliterated where a non-Roman alphabet is used in the source. While I have tried to keep to reliable sources for all my material, it should be borne in mind that the establishment of the correct meaning of a grammatical category like tense is by no means straight-forward, so that even for a language as thoroughly studied as English there remains controversy concerning the definition of the various tenses, and statements that turn out to be erroneous can be found in what are otherwise reliable and insightful sources. I hope that readers who find errors of analysis in the examples presented will communicate their objections to me. While I have carefully checked all examples against original sources, experience suggests that in a book citing examples from a wide range of languages typographical errors invariably slip past the author. I hope that readers spotting such errors will forgive me, and communicate the errors to me.

Portions of the material contained in this book have been presented at various fora, in North America, Australia, Brazil and the Netherlands, and I am grateful to all those who have offered me comments on these earlier versions of this material. I am particularly grateful to the students and guests in my seminar on Tense at the University of Southern California. For comments on a slightly earlier draft, I am grateful to John Lyons, N. V. Smith and Dieter Wunderlich. I have also benefited from general discussion with Östen Dahl. More specific acknowledgements are included in the relevant footnotes. Preparation of the pre-final draft was carried out while I was a guest at the Max-Planck-Institut für Psycholinguistik in Nijmegen.

In chapter 1, I have attempted to discuss various theoretical and methodological assumptions which underlie the body of the book (chapters 2–4). Readers who are new to the area of tense may prefer, on first reading, to skim through chapter 1 and concentrate on the more central chapters; the reasons why some of the problems discussed in chapter 1 are problems will then be clearer after the more central material has been assimilated, and this chapter can then more profitably be studied in detail.

Bernard Comrie

May 1984

1.
Some theoretical and methodological preliminaries

1.1 Scope of the work

The overall scope of this work is to provide an account of tense from the viewpoint of language universals and linguistic typology, that is, to establish the range of variation that is found across languages in tense, and what the limits are to that variation. In chapter 1, first some preliminary remarks are given concerning the notion tense and its relation to time, in particular defining tense as the grammaticalisation of location in time; this necessitates some discussion of other expressions of time in language, in particular of the conceptually distinct notion aspect, and of ways other than grammaticalisation in which location in time can be expressed in language (sections 1.2–4). The discussion of deixis in section 1.5 provides a framework of the logical possibilities for locating events in time, with discussion of which of those possibilities are found, or at least are found recurrently, across the languages of the world. Sections 1.6–7 provide further background on the problems inherent in defining the meaning of a grammatical category, with examples drawn from problems that arise in the definition of tense categories in various languages. Finally, section 8 justifies the approach taken in this book whereby tense categories have meanings that are defined independent of context, in particular discourse context, and assesses the role of discourse as a tool in establishing the meanings of tense categories.

The body of the book is composed of chapters 2 to 4, which discuss the three major parameters that are relevant in the definition of tense categories: the deictic centre (whether this is the present moment, as in absolute tense – chapter 2 – or some other point in time, as with relative tense – chapter 3); whether the event referred to is located prior to, subsequent to, or simultaneous with the deictic centre (chapters 2 and 3); and the distance in time at which the event referred to is located from the deictic centre (chapter 4). This third parameter, incidentally, is one which is omitted from most earlier accounts of tense as a grammatical category, no doubt because grammaticalisation of degrees of remoteness from the deictic centre is not found in the major European languages (e.g. distinction of a recent past from a remote past), although such distinctions are widespread among the languages of the world. At the end of each of the later chapters there is also a section showing how the parameter discussed in that chapter interacts with parameters discussed in the earlier chapters.

Chapter 5 investigates the interaction of tense with syntactic properties of various languages, showing how an adequate account of this interaction can explain apparent anomalies in the use of tense, such as examples where a given tense seems not to have its usual meaning. Special attention is paid to sequence of tenses, including the use of tenses in indirect speech.

Finally, chapter 6 ties together the discussion of the body of the book and suggests what features of this general discussion must be incorporated into a formal theory of tense. Although this chapter is much more formal than the other chapters, it is nonetheless intended as a prolegomenon to some future theory of tense rather than as a formal theory in its own right.

1.2 Time and language

For the purpose of the present book, we will assume that time can be represented as a straight line, with the past represented convention-ally to the left and the future to the right. The present moment will be represented by a point labelled o on that line (figure 1). This representation enables us to represent diagrammatically a range of ordinary-language statements about time. For instance, to say that an event occurred in the past is to locate it diagrammatically to the left of o; to say that one event occurred after another is to say that it is located diagrammatically to the right of the other event; to say that one event occurred during some other process is to say that the location of the first event is diagrammatically inside the time-span allotted to the second process (since a process necessarily takes up a certain span of time, it will be represented diagrammatically as a certain section of the time line, rather than just a point). More importantly, it will be claimed that this diagrammatic representation of time is adequate for an account of tense in human language.

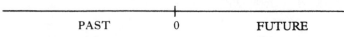

PAST   0   FUTURE

Figure 1. Representation of time

It should be noted that there are several things that are left vague, unspecified, in figure 1, and intentionally so, because they seem to have no bearing on the analysis of tense as a linguistic category (or, more generally, on linguistic expressions of time). Figure 1 is intended to leave open whether the time line is bounded at either the left (i.e. in the past) or the right (i.e. in the future); whatever stand one takes on this issue seems to be irrelevant linguistically, although it is, of course, of major philosophical importance. Figure 1 does not directly represent the flow of time, i.e. whether the present moment is viewed as moving along a stationary time line, or whether time is viewed as flowing past a stationary present reference time point. While both of these metaphors turn out to be important sources for time expressions across languages,[1] they do not seem to play any role in the characterisation of grammatical oppositions cross-linguistically. It will, however, be important for the discussion of deixis in section 1.5 and in the body of the book to note that there is motion of the present moment relative to the time line, i.e. what is now the present moment is a time point subsequent to what was the present moment five minutes ago.

Although figure 1 will probably coincide with most readers' naive conceptualisation of time, and is in accord with traditional Western philosophy, it has been claimed that some societies have radically different conceptualisations of time. Clearly, if our intention is to provide an account of tense valid for any language, then this account must not be based on culture-specific concepts of time, but should rather be a general theory appropriate to all cultures, and thus to all languages. In fact, all such claims about alternative conceptualisations of time known to me turn out either to be inaccurate, at least in terms of the relation between the alleged alternative conceptualisation and the content of figure 1, or to be irrelevant, in that they conceptualise time on such a macroscopic scale that the alternative conceptualisation turns out to be irrelevant in other than philosophical discussions about the conceptualisation of time.

The most extreme denial of figure 1 would be to claim that some cultures have absolutely no concept of time. When, however, one investigates the substance of this claim, it turns out that what is actually being claimed is considerably less than the apparent claim. One can easily see this by imagining what it would be like literally to have no conceptualisation of time. Given the conceptualisation of figure 1, we can readily express the different stages in the life of a human, i.e. that humans are first born, then grow to maturity, then age, then die. If one had no concept of time, then one would find just as natural a development where humans first appeared as dead, then came to life as old people, then grew gradually younger and eventually disappeared into their mother's womb. Equally, one would not be surprised to see a certain individual first as a grown man, then as a baby,

[1] See, for instance, Traugott (1978).

then as a corpse, then as an adolescent. Needless to say, no human culture is known to have such a conceptualisation of time.

What is true of many cultures, however, is that they seem to lack any conceptualisation of progress, i.e. in many cultures it is taken for granted that today will be much the same as yesterday, and that tomorrow, or indeed the day fifty years into the future from today, will be much the same as today. Indeed, the idea of major qualitative changes associated with the movement of time is probably a quite recent development even in Western thought: it was certainly not characteristic of most Europeans during the Middle Ages. But it is one thing to lack any concept of (or interest in) progress, and another to have no concept whatsoever of time: even if tomorrow is exactly like today, it will still be characterised by a temporal sequence whereby the sun first rises in the east, then moves across the sky, then sets in the west, rather than vice versa or arbitrarily jumping about the sky. Moreover, even in many cultures that do lack any interest in progress, there are still accounts that clearly refer to some past event, such as stories of the creation of the world, of how ancestors arrived in the area occupied by that culture, or of a golden age in the past which was considerably better than the present, or even (though much less frequently) of promised golden ages in the future.

In some instances, the claim that a certain culture lacks any concept of time, or has a radically different concept of time, is based simply on the fact that the language in question has no grammatical device for expressing location in time, i.e. has no tense (see further section 2.5). Perhaps the most famous such equivocation is in Whorf's account of Hopi, where the absence of straightforward past, present and future categories and the overriding grammatical importance of aspect and mood is taken to be indicative of a radically different conceptualisation of time.[2] It would be equally logical to assert that speakers of languages lacking grammatical gender categories have a radically different concept of sex from speakers of languages with such grammatical categories.

A more serious objection to the universality of figure 1 is that some cultures have concepts of time that are cyclic. Of course, on a limited scale all cultures necessarily have some concept of cyclicity in time, given such microscopic cycles as that of day and night, or that of the seasons of the year. However, the cultures referred to here have a macroscopic concept of cyclic time, such that the events that are happening at the present moment are direct reflections of events that occurred in a previous cycle, and will in turn

---

[2] Carroll (1956); for a thorough refutation of Whorf's views on Hopi time, see Malotki (1983).

be reflected by the events in each subsequent cycle. This might suggest replacing figure 1 with a circle for such cultures, which include Australian Aboriginal cultures. This assumption would, however, be incorrect. The most obvious reason, given our present concerns, is that no language has been found in which such a macroscopic concept of time cycles has any relevance to the expression of tense as a grammatical category. In the body of this book various examples from Australian Aboriginal languages are cited, and in no single example do we find grammatical categories whose meaning would be definable in such terms as 'occurring at the present moment or the equivalent point in any other cycle', rather, we find categories definable in such terms as 'occurring at the present moment', just as in cultures which lack cyclic concepts of time on a macroscopic level. In fact, in cultures which have such a cyclic conceptualisation of time, the cycles are invariably of such long duration that it makes no difference to the activities of daily life that they are taking place in a cycle of time rather than on a straight time line. In other words, this difference in conceptualisation of time overall is no more relevant to a study of tense than would be the difference between Euclidean and non-Euclidean geometry to a study of the meaning of terms like *here* and *there*. Moreover, even in societies that have a cyclic concept of time, the individual cycles seem to be viewed as chronologically arranged, i.e. there are earlier cycles and later cycles, so that at best the cyclicity would be superimposed on an overall conceptualisation of time that is linear. The conclusion is, thus, that figure 1 is an adequate representation of time for the purpose of analysing expressions of time in natural language.

Our interest in this book will be to relate various events, processes, states, etc., to the time line represented in figure 1. Rather than repeating at each occurrence the expression processes, events, states, etc., it will be convenient to have a single term to subsume all of these, and this term will be *situation*. It should be noted that this is therefore a technical term, with a considerably broader meaning than the corresponding word in ordinary English. Situations which are punctual, or at least which are conceived as such, will be represented by points on the time line. Situations which occupy, or are conceived as occupying, a certain stretch of time will be represented as stretches of the time line. Thus, in figure 2 situation A precedes situation B, while situation C follows situation B; situations D and

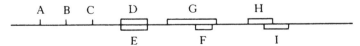

Figure 2. Representation of situations on the time-line

E overlap, as do F and G, and also H and I, although the precise natures of the overlaps are somewhat different (D and E cover exactly the same time stretch; F occurs wholly within G; part of the time stretch of H is also part of the time stretch of I, while there is also part of the time stretch of H that is not part of I and part of I that is not part of H). For easier legibility, situations have been represented graphically above or below the time line, but it should be borne in mind that more accurately they should be thought of as on the line. In figure 2, there is no specification of the present moment, so that we can talk about the location of situations A–I relative to each other, but not in more absolute terms, relative to the present moment. Figure 3 adds specification of the present moment, so that we can now say that A, B, C, D, and E are in the past; F, H and I in the future; while G includes the present moment, i.e. is currently ongoing.

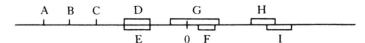

Figure 3. Representation of situations relative to the present moment

There are basically two ways in which one can relate a situation to the time line. One is to locate the situation somewhere on the time line, necessarily in relation to some other specified point or segment of the line, since in one sense all time location is relative, there being no absolutely specified points. (The use of the term absolute tense to refer to locating events relative to the present moment is merely a terminological convention.) This concept of time location is essential to the linguistic category of tense, as will be made clearer in section 1.3.

The second possibility for relating situations to the time line is that one might be interested in discussing the internal temporal contour of a situation, for instance in discussing whether it is to be represented as a point on the time line, or as a stretch of the time line. The internal temporal contour of a situation provides the conceptual basis for the notion of aspect, which refers to the grammaticalisation of expression of internal temporal constituency. Thus the difference between *John was singing* and *John is singing* in English is one of tense, namely a location before the present moment versus a location including the present moment; while the difference between *John was singing* and *John sang* is one of aspect. The phenomenon of aspect will not be further treated, other than incidentally, in this book.[3] The reader should, however, beware that in many linguistic works, especially traditional grammars, the term tense is rather mislead-

[3] For this author's views on aspect, see Comrie (1976).

ingly used to cover both tense and aspect, as when Spanish, for instance, is said to distinguish a preterite tense (e.g. *hablé* 'I spoke') from an imperfect tense (e.g. *hablaba* 'I used to speak, I was speaking'). Given the current widespread acceptance of the opposition between the terms tense and aspect, it is advisable to make the terminological distinction in order to avoid conceptual confusion.[4] The problem is exacerbated by the fact that many languages have forms that include specification both of location in time and of internal temporal contour; thus Spanish *hablé* is both perfective aspect and past tense. Nonetheless, it is crucial to maintain the conceptual distinction between tense and aspect, and to have a terminology that is capable of maintaining this distinction. For the treatment of forms that combine tense and aspect (or other category sets), refer to section 1.4.

1.3 Location in time

The idea of locating situations in time is a purely conceptual notion, and is as such potentially independent of the range of distinctions made in any particular language. It does, however, seem to be the case that all human languages have ways of locating in time. They differ from one another, however, on two parameters. The first, and overall less interesting for our present purpose, is the degree of accuracy of temporal location that is achievable in different languages. The second, and more important, is the way in which situations are located in time, in particular the relative weight assigned to the lexicon and to the grammar in establishing location in time.

In modern technological societies, we are accustomed to very accurate specifications of time location and of other phenomena relating to time, so that not only has the time unit *second* become entrenched, but many members of the culture are at home in talking of much smaller stretches of time, such as nanoseconds. Given these possibilities, very fine distinctions in location of time are possible, and when the linguistic possibilities are combined with those of standard mathematical notation an infinite degree of precision is in principle attainable. In many other cultures, however, such precision is not attainable, at least not by means other than direct borrowing of expressions from the languages of more technological cultures. Indeed, in some cultures, very little value is attached to precision

[4] In the grammars of some languages, moreover, the term tense has an even wider range of use. For instance, many Bantu languages are described as having special 'tenses' for use in relative clauses, and special negative 'tenses', thus giving a fourfold multiplication of the number of tenses (main clause, main clause negative, relative clause, relative clause negative). Needless to say, the difference between corresponding affirmative and negative, or main clause and relative clause, forms is not one of tense, and it would be wise to avoid this terminological confusion.

in temporal location, so that in Yidiny, for example, it is impossible to distinguish lexically between the concepts 'today' and 'now'.[5] Although, in cultures where precise location in time is attainable, expressions can be created for such precise statements, it should be noted that such expressions do not impinge at all on the grammar of the language in question, rather they use existing grammatical patterns, at best creating new lexical items (such as *nanosecond*), or even making use of existing lexical items and mathematical expressions in order to gain precision (e.g. 10^{-6} *seconds*). No language has grammatical devices to make such fine locations, and indeed the languages of the cultures that find it necessary to make such fine discriminations characteristically have a very small range of grammatical distinctions in this area: thus, in English, it is possible to locate a situation before the present moment (by using the past tense), and even to locate a further situation prior to that first situation (by using the pluperfect), but there is no way of quantifying grammatically the time lapse between the first and second situations, or between either of them and the present moment.

The sum total of expressions for locating in time can be divided, in terms of their importance for the structure of the language, into three classes. (The same classification is, of course, possible for other notional oppositions, such as those of aspect or number.) The largest set is that composed of *lexically composite expressions*, since this set is potentially infinite in a language that has linguistic means for measuring time intervals; this gives English expressions of the type *five minutes after John left, 10^{-45} seconds after the Big Bang*, which simply involve slotting more accurate time specifications into the positions of a syntactic expression. The second set is the set of *lexical items* in the language that express location in time, and would include such items as *now, today, yesterday*. The precise dividing line between lexically composite expressions and lexical items is different from language to language: thus, English *last year* is a lexically composite expression, whose meaning can be calculated compositionally from the meaning of *last* and the meaning of *year*, whereas the Czech equivalent *loni* is a single lexical item. Since the stock of items listed in the lexicon is necessarily finite, the range of distinctions possible lexically is necessarily smaller than that which is possible using lexically composite expressions.

The third set is the set of *grammatical categories*, which turns out to be the least sensitive of the three. Thus English, for instance, has at most the following grammaticalised expressions of location in time: present, past, future, pluperfect, future perfect, and many linguists would even question the inclusion of the future (and, presumably, the future perfect) in this list.

[5] Dixon (1977: 498–499).

While many languages have more tense categories than English, in particular languages that distinguish degrees of remoteness in past and future (chapter 4), even the maximal system would have at most tens of categories, rather than the several orders of magnitude more possible in the lexicon. The analogy with number is interesting here: English has grammatically only a two-way opposition (singular and plural); lexically there are around thirty items (excluding those restricted to mathematical or scientific contexts); while for many speakers the possibilities for lexically composite expressions are infinite.

1.4 Tense as grammaticalised location in time

The basis of the discussion in the body of this book is that tense is grammaticalised expression of location in time. On the one hand, this can be viewed as purely definitional. In this way, we would look at a particular form in a language, decide whether it does in fact express location in time and whether it is indeed a grammatical category, and then pronounce it to be tense or not. The definition would enable us, for instance, to say that the difference between *John sang* and *John sings* in English is one of tense, whereas that between *John sings* and *John is singing* is not, but rather of aspect. However, there are two respects in which our view of tense as grammaticalised location in time is more than purely definitional.

First, it is conceivable that, using the above definition of tense, we might examine grammatical categories across languages and find that there are none which match the definition, i.e. we might be forced to the conclusion that tense does not exist, and should therefore not be part of linguistic theory. It is therefore an empirical claim of this book that tense does exist, i.e. that there are languages which express location in time by means of grammatical categories. Indeed, given that no restrictions are placed by the definition on what kind of location in time is to be considered, it is probable that most of the world's languages will turn out to have tense, although there will still probably remain a small residue of languages that do not (section 2.5), just as there are some languages with no grammatical category of aspect or number.

Secondly, it will emerge from the discussion in the body of the book that there are very heavy constraints that language imposes on the range of expressions of location in time that can be grammaticalised. In fact, all clear instances of tense cross-linguistically can be represented in terms of the notions of deictic centre (section 1.5), location at, before, or after the deictic centre, and distance from the deictic centre; furthermore, the location of the deictic centre relative to the present moment is constrained in the same

9

way as the location of a situation relative to the deictic centre. Given the wealth of logically conceivable contrasts in time location, or even those that are known to be lexicalised across languages, this is a very small range indeed. Thus the definition given above permits a highly constrained theory of tense.

Before examining further differences between kinds of location in time that can be grammaticalised versus those that can be lexicalised, it will be useful to include some further discussion on the distinction between grammaticalisation and lexicalisation in general. This discussion will not be entirely conclusive, since there still remains considerable controversy surrounding the precise borderline between grammatical and lexical categories.[6] The simplest statement of the difference would be to say that grammaticalisation refers to integration into the grammatical system of a language, while lexicalisation refers merely to integration into the lexicon of the language, without any necessary repercussions on its grammatical structure. While this circular definition is surprisingly successful in getting people to appreciate the distinction between grammaticalisation and lexicalisation, clearly some characterisation in independent terms would be preferable. The suggestion advanced here is that the difference can be understood in terms of the interaction of two parameters: that of obligatory expression, and that of morphological boundness. The clearest instances of grammaticalisation satisfy both these criteria (they are obligatory and morphologically bound), the clearest instances of lexicalisation satisfy neither, while there will be many borderline cases which the criteria do not assign unequivocally to grammaticalisation or lexicalisation.[7]

The English past/non-past opposition is a clear instance of a grammaticalised opposition. It is quite impossible to construct an English sentence containing a finite verb that is neutral as between the two poles of this opposition, i.e. *John runs* is clearly non-past, and *John ran* is clearly past, and there is no third term that is neither. Moreover the expression of the distinction is by means of bound morphemes (taken to include morphophonemic alternation, i.e. anything that does not involve a separate word). However, obligatoriness is not in itself a sufficient criterion for assigning an opposition grammatical status. In Norwegian, for instance, expression of the subject by means of a noun phrase is obligatory, as in *jeg kommer* 'I come', *du kommer* 'you come', *han kommer* 'he comes', but it

---

[6] See further Lyons (1977: 234–237).

[7] The definition is thus a prototype definition, rather than a definition in terms of necessary-and-sufficient conditions. Readers unfamiliar with this distinction should refer to section 1.6.

would be a gross distortion of the traditional concept to argue that Norwegian thereby has a grammatical category of person and number, since Norwegian verbs, unlike those of English, do not change for the person and number of the subject (cf. English *I come* but *he comes*). The crucial difference between Norwegian and English is that in English the person and number of the subject do have repercussions on the grammar (via the rule of subject–verb agreement), whereas in Norwegian there is no such interaction.

But morphological boundness is not in itself a necessary criterion. In Bamileke-Dschang, for instance, tense is expressed primarily by means of auxiliaries, which are not bound morphemes, as in the distinction between *à kè táŋ'ŋ́* 'he bargained yesterday', *à lè táŋ'ŋ́* 'he bargained some days ago', and *à lè láʔ ŋ́'táŋ* 'he bargained a long time ago'.[8] However, although the English glosses use lexical items (like *yesterday*) and lexically composite expressions (like *a long time ago*), in Bamileke-Dschang it is obligatory to make the distinctions outlined above, whereas in English one could refer to all of these situations by saying simply *he bargained*; moreover, the auxiliaries used in the Bamileke-Dschang examples are not separate lexical items, so that one cannot account for the meanings assigned to the sentences above in terms of composition of the meanings of separate lexical items.

The above was an attempt at a definition of the difference between grammaticalisation and lexicalisation, with special reference to location in time. In addition, there is a major distinction between the kinds of location in time concepts that are characteristically grammaticalised, versus those that are characteristically lexicalised. The notions that are most commonly grammaticalised across the languages of the world are simple anteriority, simultaneity, and posteriority, i.e. with the present moment as deictic centre, past, present and future. It is rare to find lexical items with such general semantic characterisations, except for *now* in its relation to the present. While adverbials like English *formerly* might seem a good lexical substitute for the past tense, further investigation shows that their distribution is rather different, in particular *formerly* cannot be used to refer to a single event in the past (i.e. one cannot say *formerly John hit Bill* to mean that on some occasion in the past, John hit Bill) – *formerly* has, in addition to past location in time, also a habitual aspectual component. English expressions like *in the past, in the future,* are merely parasitic on the metalanguage of tense.

Conversely, it is rare to find tenses that are as specific as lexical items with time reference in language, again with the exception of present tense and *now*. While there are some languages with a tense (yesterday past tense)

[8] For the data, see Hyman (1980).

corresponding exactly to the lexical item 'yesterday' (chapter 4), such specificity in the grammatical system is unusual: even in languages with different degrees of remoteness in past and future, the boundaries between the grammatical categories are usually much more fluid than those between lexical items. And no language seems to have a special tense for last year, comparable to the Czech lexical item *loni* mentioned above.

Going beyond the synchronic analysis of languages, another striking piece of evidence for the difference between grammaticalisation and lexicalisation of location of time is that there are hardly any good attestations of grammatical tense marking deriving from lexical items that express time location (whereas there are numerous attestations, for instance, of tense markers deriving from or giving rise to aspect and mood markers). The only examples known to me are the development of tense markers in some Kru languages from time adverbials; the development of a future tense marker *bai, baimbai, bambai*, in New Guinea Pidgin English from the English adverbial *by and by*; and the development of the yesterday past tense suffix *-ngul* from the lexical item *ngul* 'yesterday' in Kalaw Lagaw Ya.[9]

So far, we have spoken of tense as being a grammatical category, but without saying what it is a grammatical category of. In most languages that have tense, tense is indicated on the verb, either by the verb morphology (as with English past *loved* versus non-past *loves*), or by grammatical words adjacent to the verb, as with the auxiliaries referred to above in the Bamileke-Dschang examples. In a few languages, tense marking, or at least some tense marking, takes place in the position reserved for sentence-particles; thus in Warlpiri, tense is indicated as part of the auxiliary complex that stands in sentence-second position.[10] While much traditional grammar regards tense as a category of the verb on the basis of its morphological attachment to the verb, more recently it has been argued that tense should be regarded as a category of the whole sentence, or in logical terms of the whole proposition, since it is the truth-value of the proposition as a whole, rather than just some property of the verb, that must be matched against the state of the world at the appropriate time point.[11]

Even more recently, however, there have been suggestions that the earlier analysis, assigning tense to the verb, may be correct, though for reasons that were not considered by those who set up the original model.[12]

[9] For Kru languages, see Marchese (1984). For Kalaw Lagaw Ya (Mabuiag dialect), see Bani & Klokeid (1972: 98); note however that the suffix of the Mabuiag last night past tense, *-bungel*, bears no resemblance to the adverbial *kubila* 'last night'.

[10] Hale (1973).

[11] See, for instance, Lyons (1977: 678).

[12] Enç (1981).

The reason is that the noun phrase arguments of a verb are very often outside the scope of the tense, whereas the verb is necessarily within the scope of the tense. Thus, an example like *by 1990, every postgraduate student will have met a prime minister* is true if, by the stipulated time point, everyone who is now a postgraduate student will have met someone who before or during 1990 will have held the position of prime minister. In particular, it is not necessary that the person meeting the prime minister should be a postgraduate student at the time he meets the prime minister; nor is it necessary that the person met by the postgraduate student should be prime minister at the time of the meeting. One of the instances of a relevant meeting would be that between John, who is now a postgraduate student, and Mr Wilson in 1979, even though John was then only an undergraduate and Mr Wilson was no longer prime minister. Under the tense as a sentential category analysis, the tendency for tense indicators to adhere to the verb has to be explained in terms of the verb's being head of the sentence, whereas under the analysis whereby tense is a category of the verb the adherence of tense to the verb falls out without any further specification.

Although tense is primarily a category of the verb or of the sentence, one occasionally finds tense expressed elsewhere or with a different domain. In Malagasy, for instance, certain spatial and temporal adverbs obligatorily agree in tense with the verb, so that the word for 'here' is *ao* in the present but *t-ao* in the past, thus giving *n-ianatra t-ao (*ao) i Paoly omaly* 'Paul studied here yesterday', where *n-* is the past tense prefix on the verb. Note that semantically, however, tense is not a property of these adverbs, but rather of the verb or the sentence.[13] In Nootka, tense can be shown on noun phrases, thus distinguishing 'the entity that was an X' from 'the entity that is an X', as in *inikw-ihl-'minih-'is-it-'i* 'fire in: house plural diminutive past nominal', i.e. 'the former small fires in the house'.[14] It should be noted, however, that English expressions like *ex-president* have a narrower semantic range than *person who was a president*: the former, but not the latter, excludes the possibility of this person still being president.

1.5 Tense and deixis

Time itself does not provide any landmarks in terms of which one can locate situations. If time had a beginning, we do not know where that beginning was, so we cannot locate anything else relative to that beginning (other than, trivially, by saying that the situation is posterior to that beginning). If time has an end, again we do not know its location, so

[13] Randriamasimanana (1981: 355–367).
[14] Sapir (1921: 133–134).

again no non-trivial location is possible relative to that endpoint. Therefore, it is necessary to establish some arbitrary reference point, with reference to which we can then locate situations in time. In principle, a number of logical possibilities for reference points are available, and for lexically composite expressions many of these are used in language. Thus our own calendrical system chooses as its arbitrary reference point the (traditional) date for Christ's birth, and counts years backwards and forwards from this time point; in ancient Rome the equivalent reference point was the (traditional) date for the founding of the city of Rome (753 B.C.). One possibility for a reference point is therefore a 'famous event'. Although this possibility is actualised for lexically composite expressions, and even to a certain extent for lexical items (cf. *pre-Revolutionary, post-Reformation*), it is apparently never used for tense as a grammatical category, or indeed for grammatical categories of any kind.

What one rather finds most typically is the choice of the speech situation as the reference point, i.e. the present moment (for time), the present spot (for space), and the speaker and hearer (for person). As far as tense is concerned, then, the reference point is typically the present moment, and tenses locate situations either at the same time as the present moment (or perhaps including the present moment – see section 2.1), or prior to the present moment, or subsequent to the present moment, with further potential categories if degrees of remoteness from the present moment are distinguished grammatically.

A system which relates entities to a reference point is termed a deictic system, and we can therefore say that tense is deictic.[15] (By contrast, aspect is non-deictic, since discussion of the internal temporal constituency of a situation is quite independent of its relation to any other time point.)

The most straightforward instance of a deictic system is one where the 'here and now', i.e. the speech situation, is taken as deictic centre. In terms of person, this defines first person as the speaker and second person as the hearer, with everything else being third person. In terms of place, the place where the speech situation takes place is defined as *here*, everywhere else as *there*. In fact, the situation is somewhat more complex for place, since the physical location of speaker and hearer can never be absolutely identical, and it is possible that there may be considerable physical separation between them. In English, *here* refers more specifically to the location of the speaker, so that if the hearer is physically separated from the speaker the hearer's physical location will be referred to as *there*. Some languages make a three-way distinction, e.g. Tuscan Italian *qui* 'here' (by me), *costí* 'there'

[15] For general discussion of deixis, see Fillmore (1975), Lyons (1977: ch. 15).

(by you), *là* 'there' (away from both of us). In English, the deictic verb *come*, indicating motion towards the deictic centre, treats both the speaker's location and the hearer's location as deictic centre, even when they are physically separated, so that one can say both *you will come to me* and *I will come to you*; Spanish *venir* 'to come', by contrast, can only treat the speaker's location as deictic centre, so that the Spanish for 'I'm coming' (sc. to you) is *voy*, literally 'I go'.

Although location in time is in many ways similar to location in space, and the expressions used in languages for location in time are often derived etymologically from spatial expressions,[16] there are some crucial distinctions that should be noted at this point. First, as far as space is concerned, not-here defines a continuous area, i.e. everything which is not the location of the speech situation (or, more narrowly, of the speaker). For location in time, however, because of the one-dimensional nature of time, not-now does not define a continuous area, but rather the discontinuous area consisting of past and future, but separated by the present moment. Languages do often have lexical items referring to not-now, such as English *then* 'at that time', i.e. at some time other than now, but grammaticalisation of not-now as a single tense seems not to exist as a possibility, despite the widespread grammaticalisation of now as present tense, and the existence of past and future tenses. (Conversely, since space is three-dimensional, there is no absolute spatial analogue to the past/future distinction in time, although to some extent the back/front distinction, even though dependent on an arbitrary spatial orientation, has similar properties, including similar lexical expression in many languages.)

A second distinction between deixis with regard to space and with regard to time is that, in general, the present moment is the same for both speaker and hearer, whereas for space it is possible for speaker and hearer to be in different locations and still communicate – indeed, strictly, they must be in different locations. While modern technology has vastly increased the possibilities for spatial dislocation of speaker and hearer, even pre-technological societies have frequent situations where speaker and hearer are located in significantly different spots, e.g. when the speaker wants to call the hearer to him, or when people are shouting to one another from one hill-top to another; it is therefore not surprising that many languages should have separate grammatical categories or lexical items taking either the speaker or the hearer as deictic centre.

For time, however, it is only the relatively recent invention of writing, and the even more recent invention of sound recordings, that have enabled

16 Traugott (1978).

temporal dislocation of speaker and hearer, and human language apparently still operates on the assumption that the temporal deictic centre is the same for both speaker and hearer. Apparently no language has two words for 'now', one referring to the moment when the writer is composing his letter and the other to the moment when the reader is deciphering it, nor does any language have distinctions in tense system to specify this difference. On road signs and other such notices, the deictic centre is simply taken to be that of the hearer, as in *you are now leaving West Berlin*, where the sign may have been painted years before the traveller reading it leaves West Berlin. For letters and similar communications, some cultures have developed rules as to which deictic centre, the speaker's or the hearer's, should be used, but these do not impinge upon the grammar of the language. Thus Roman society, presumably for reasons of politeness, recommended use of the recipient's deictic centre, so that Cicero could write to Atticus *cum mihi dīxisset Caecilius puerum sē Rōmam mittere, haec scrīpsī raptim* 'since Caecilius has told [literally: had told] me that he is sending a servant-boy to Rome, I write [literally: wrote] this in a hurry', although it was apparently not unusual to lapse into the speaker's deictic centre in the middle of the letter.[17] But as far as the lexicon and the grammar are concerned, language makes the assumption that there is only one deictic centre common to speaker and hearer.

Although the speech situation, the 'here and now', is the most basic deictic centre, it is possible to have other deictic centres, provided these are clarified by the context. Thus, with regard to spatial deixis in English, the verb *come* usually refers to the location of either the speaker or the hearer. However, if some other location is indicated as deictic centre, then this location can serve as the end-point of the action referred to by *come*; for instance, in a description of a journey to Canterbury one could say *and at last we came to Canterbury*, even though this refers to the location of neither speaker nor hearer. Indeed, one can even use this to refer to the end of a journey being undertaken by some third person to a location where neither speaker nor hearer is located, as in *and at last Marco Polo came to Peking*. The existence of deictic centres other than the present moment will play a crucial role in the discussion of relative tense in chapter 3. In the meantime, it may be noted that non-finite verb forms in English often have relative time reference, i.e. time reference relative to a deictic centre other than the present moment. Thus, in *those sitting on the benches were forced to move*, one possible interpretation of the time reference of *sitting* is as

---

[17] Gildersleeve & Lodge (1895: § 252).

simultaneous with (or overlapping) that of *were forced to move*, i.e. the present participle indicates present time reference, but with respect to a reference point which is in the past (given the past tense of *were forced*). What is crucial to all tense specifications, however, is the need for a deictic centre or reference point. (In chapter 3, it will be shown that some tenses require specification of more than one reference point.)

So far, we have assumed that the deictic centre for tense will be a single point in time. The question therefore arises whether all tenses can be described in terms of such deictic centres (or, possibly, combinations of such deictic centres, for tenses requiring more than one reference point). Certainly, for most tenses in most languages, and for those tenses which seem to be at the core of the tense system in any language, this turns out to be true. However, there are some forms on the periphery of tense systems that should be discussed, even though they will not be incorporated into the overall structure of the body of the book. These are instances where some situation is located relative to some cyclically recurring event, of which the ones known to me to be relevant are different parts of the 24-hour cycle, i.e. morning, afternoon, evening, day, night. Clearly, location relative to such cyclically recurring events is possible by means of lexically composite expressions, as when a certain situation is said to take place *by day*, or *at night*, or *every morning*, or *this morning*. Moreover, some languages do indeed have bound morphemes, attachable to the verb, which indicate the time of day at which a situation holds: the precise interpretation (e.g. as 'this morning', or 'some morning in the past', or 'every morning') will depend on the tense and aspect of the verb, or on context if these are insufficient to make this specification. Such morphemes are found in a number of Australian languages (e.g. Yandruwandha, Tiwi), and in the West African language Kom. In all of these examples, the indicator of cyclic time is clearly a bound morpheme, but in none of these instances is expression of time of day obligatory. In Tiwi there are several incorporated forms of nouns which occur only bound to a following verb stem, and such incorporated forms are often quite distinct from that of the closest corresponding separate lexical item, e.g. *puniŋkapa* 'meat', but *ji-mən-alipi-aŋkina* 'he me meat steal', i.e. 'he stole my meat', so it is perhaps not too surprising to find the bound morphemes *atə-* 'in the morning' and *kə-* 'in the evening', radically different from the lexical items *tapinaɟi* (archaic: *aɟawari*) 'morning' and *tapini* 'evening'. Yandruwandha and Kom, however, do not otherwise have such suppletive incorporation, so it is all the more surprising to find the Yandruwandha suffixes *-nina* 'by day', *-talka* (and perhaps *-warrka*) 'in the morning' and *-yukarra* 'at night', and the

Kom affix *lè* 'in the morning'.[18] Given the rarity of such morphemes across the languages of the world, and the fact that they are always optional, whereas many languages (including these languages) have obligatory tense indication with non-cyclic deictic centres, we shall assume that they occupy at best a peripheral status in the overall typology of tense, and leave them out of account for the remainder of the discussion. It remains an open question whether a more adequate general account of tense could be constructed including them.

It is also worth noting at this point that there are apparently no languages that have a specific tense to refer to a culturally defined 'special period', such as a golden age, despite the importance of such special periods in many cultures. Some cultures do have conventions as to which tense should be used in speaking of events from such a special period – thus Gumatj requires use of the more recent past tense in referring to events that took place in the dream-time[19] – but these are always tenses that have other uses in addition to this culturally specific use.

1.6 Basic and secondary meanings

So far, we have spoken rather glibly about assigning meanings to grammatical categories, and it is now time to look more seriously into the problems that arise in attempting to carry out this programme. In fact, these problems are far from trivial, and the discussion of the core of this book will largely stand or fall by the appropriateness of the solution adopted to this particular problem overall and in individual cases.

The strongest theory would be to claim that, for each tense (and more generally, for each grammatical category, lexical item, and perhaps syntactic construction), one can establish a set of necessary and sufficient conditions such that every permitted use of the form will be allowed by these conditions, and every rejected use of the form will be disallowed by these conditions. In different contexts, the form in question might be given different interpretations, but these would always be predictable on the basis of the interaction of the meaning of the item (as given by the necessary and sufficient conditions) with features of the context, i.e. the meaning itself would be invariable. Although this brave programme has been undertaken with regard to the meanings of tense, specifically, in the present work a more flexible approach is adopted.[20] This is not because of a general belief

---

[18] The source for the Tiwi material is Osborne (1974: 45–46, 47–50); for Yandruwandha, Breen (1976); and for Kom, Hyman (1980: 234–235). See also the discussion of Burera in chapter 4.

[19] Joyce Ross (personal communication).

[20] For such an attempt, see Joos (1964); cf. the criticism by Woisetschlaeger (1977: 105–107)

that less strict theories are preferable to stricter theories – quite the contrary – but rather because of a belief that in the characterisation of the meanings of tense (and probably many other linguistic categories and items), the more flexible approach provides a more accurate characterisation of the linguistic system. The approach followed in this book does, however, retain the distinction between a context-independent meaning and interpretation fostered by specific contexts (see section 1.8). However, it is acknowledged that a given grammatical category may have more than one meaning (it is thus logically possible that the auxiliary *will* in English might have both temporal and modal meanings); that a grammatical category may have a basic meaning and a number of peripheral meanings or uses (where these are not predictable from the interaction of basic meaning and context); and that the basic meaning of a lexical item may be definable in terms of a prototype, i.e. in terms of the most characteristic instance, rather than in terms of necessary-and-sufficient conditions. These three points are often interrelated, and will be illustrated by the following examples.

When an analysis of a given grammatical category as being tense is advanced, it is often objected that this grammatical category has certain uses which are not subsumed by, and may even be contradictory to, the definition in terms of location in time. The English past will serve as an example here. Although most uses of the English past tense do serve to locate situations prior to the present moment, there are several uses that do not. One is in counterfactuals, e.g. *if you did this I would be very happy*, where *did* clearly does not have past time reference, but refers rather to a potential action in the present or future. For some speakers of English, there is a distinction between the form of the verb *be* used in such constructions and the form of the verb used with past time reference – cf. *John was here* (past time reference), but *if John were here* (counterfactual present) – so that one might argue that here we are simply dealing with two distinct but homophonous (for most verbs, or, for some speakers, for all verbs) forms. However, this cannot be applied to the use of the past tense in polite requests, as in *I just wanted to ask you if you could lend me a pound*, which in most circumstances is unlikely to be intended or to be interpreted as a report on the speaker's desires in the past, but rather as an expression of a present desire to borrow some money. The function of the past tense in this example is to indicate politeness: the version given is more polite than *I just want to ask you if you could lend me a pound*. The existence of such

who, despite his general commitment to univocality (i.e. assignment of a single meaning to a single grammatical category), modifies this principle to allow for a specifiable list of exceptions.

counterexamples to the general characterisation of the English past as indicating past time reference does not invalidate this general characterisation, given the distinction adopted here between basic and secondary meanings: past time reference is the basic meaning of the past tense, while politeness is a secondary meaning (or, perhaps more accurately, use) of this same form.

In order to abandon the characterisation of the English past as indicating basically past time reference, it would be necessary to show that there is some alternative characterisation of its meaning from which past time reference, as well as politeness (and perhaps present counterfactuality) would all fall out automatically as special cases. Suggestions that have been made in the literature strike me as either incorrect (if interpreted literally) or as too vague to be testable. In particular, this would cover attempts to define the overall meaning of the English past tense as non-actuality. First, many instances of non-actuality are not referred to using the past tense, as in open conditions (e.g. *if you want to go, you can*), where there is no commitment to your wanting to go as being actual. Secondly, many instances of the past tense are not non-actual: the polite request above still expresses an actual desire.

Other languages provide similar examples. In Norwegian, for example, it is possible to use the past tense to express a present surprise or other affective connotation, e.g. *detta smakte godt* 'this tastes [literally: tasted] good'.[21] In German, it is possible to use the past tense in such expressions as *wer bekam die Gulaschsuppe?*, literally 'who received the goulash soup?', said by a waiter who has brought the orders to a table and wishes to be reminded who ordered this particular dish; clearly there is no sense in which *bekam* 'received' has literal past time reference here, given that the diner has not yet received his order of goulash soup.[22] But equally there is no obvious way in which these Norwegian or German examples can be integrated into a single more general account of the past tense other than past time reference.

In several languages, the past tense can be used for imminent future events. Thus in Russian, the usual expression for use when one is about to leave is *ja pošel*, literally 'I left' even though this is clearly not literally true. Incidentally, one cannot incorporate this example by saying that the deictic centre for use of the past in Russian is a time point slightly after the present moment, rather than the present moment itself, because this would then work havoc with the rest of the tense system, making it, for instance, incomprehensible why the present, rather than the past, is used for

[21] Vannebo (1979: 176–179).　　[22] Wunderlich (1970: 139–140).

currently ongoing processes. Rather, it seems that such uses of the past should simply be treated as exceptions. It may be noted that English has similar tense-time reference discrepancy here in the use of *I'm coming* in response to a call before one has actually set out, a discrepancy which is even greater in French *j'y suis*, 'I'm there', which would suggest literally that I have not only set out already but already reached my destination. With these examples, one can readily present a rationalisation for the non-literal use of the past tense, as an indication of the imminence of the future situation – it is as if it were already present – but this rationalisation does not remove the discrepancy between the literal meaning of the utterance and the context to which it is applied. This is not to belittle such rationalisations: they certainly form part of the explanation as to why this discrepancy is tolerated (in conjunction with Gricean conversational principles – see section 1.7), and it would form an interesting study to ascertain how grammatical categories and other linguistic items come to develop secondary uses in addition to their basic meaning, but this falls outside the scope of the present investigation.

The examples just discussed are instances where it is reasonably clear which of the various uses of the given grammatical form should be taken as the basic meaning. There are other examples, however, where this distinction is much less clear-cut. One such is the characterisation of the so-called future tense in English, which can certainly be used to indicate future time reference, as in *it will rain tomorrow*, but can also be used to make predictions about other times, e.g. the present, as in *it will be raining already* (said by someone who had noticed the storm-clouds gathering, but has not yet actually ascertained that it is already raining), in addition to various other modal uses, as in *he will go swimming in dangerous waters*, i.e. 'he insists on going swimming', *will you do this for me?*, i.e. 'are you willing to do this for me?'. Great controversy has surrounded the question whether the future (i.e. the form with the auxiliary *will*) should be given a single characterisation that captures both its temporal and its modal uses; or whether it should be considered basically a tense with secondary modal uses, or basically a mood with secondary temporal uses; or whether it should simply be said to have two sets of meanings, temporal and modal, with neither being dominant. We return to this question in section 2.3, although without definitively resolving the problem.

Another set of problematic instances concerns the relationship between absolute and relative time reference for many tenses (see further section 3.1). With the English non-finite verb forms, it seems in general clear that they have basically relative time reference, i.e. time reference defined relative to some deictic centre established by the context, so that the primary interpretation of *those sitting on the benches were asked to leave* is as 'those who were (at that time) sitting on the benches were asked to leave'. There is a secondary interpretation, as 'those who are (now) sitting on the benches were (then) asked to leave', where the non-finite verb form is apparently interpreted absolutely, with the present moment as the deictic centre. But in fact both these interpretations can be subsumed under relative tense once one realises that one of the possible deictic centres for a relative tense is the present moment, especially when the context does not suggest any other reference point. In languages which have just a single set of forms, with no distinction between some forms that are invariably absolute and those that are invariably relative, as with the distinction between finite and non-finite forms in English, it is often difficult to decide whether the tenses are basically given absolute time reference, with relative time reference a secondary interpretation for certain contexts; or whether the tenses should be analysed as basically relative tense, with the apparent absolute time reference interpretation being a context-specific interpretation, in particular in a context where no other deictic centre is specified. The Arabic tense-aspect system would be an instance in question (see further section 3.1).

Related to the question of basic versus secondary meanings is the question of whether the definition of a category should be given in terms of necessary-and-sufficient conditions or in terms of a prototype. The former kind of definition establishes strict criteria for deciding whether a given entity belongs to the set being described or not, without differentiating among entities that do belong to the set, i.e. it sets up a clear dividing line between what is a member of the set and what is not a member of the set. By contrast, a definition in terms of prototypes characterises a most typical member of the set, and other entities can then be classified in terms of their degree of similarity to or difference from this prototypical set-member. A prototype definition thus does not establish a clear boundary to a set, since set membership is a question of degree rather than an all-or-none decision; similarly, even among entities that are close to the prototypical member of the set, there is still differentiation in terms of more and less close correspondence to the prototype. A good illustration of the need for a prototype definition of concepts is the definition of colour terms: there is no clear-cut boundary separating, for instance, *blue* from *purple*, but there are colours that are clearly good values for each of these concepts, along with many other colours that are not readily assignable to one or the other.

In most of the discussion in this book, the difference between definitions in terms of necessary-and-sufficient conditions and in terms of prototypes will not play a significant role. There is, however, one area where the use of prototype definitions is crucial, namely in the characterisation of degrees of remoteness in past and future (see further chapter 4). If we look at complex systems of degrees of temporal remoteness, as for instance in Bamileke-Dschang, then we often find that the characterisations of the various tenses leave apparent temporal gaps, i.e. degrees of remoteness which it is impossible to express in the language concerned. Thus, in Bamileke-Dschang one past tense, P_4, is described as referring to situations that happened 'the day before yesterday or a few days earlier', while the adjacent past tense P_5 is described as referring to situations 'separated from today by a year or more'. This apparently leaves a gap from a few days ago to a year ago where there is no appropriate grammatical form in Bamileke-Dschang. The absurdity of this conclusion disappears once one realises that the characterisations given of the tenses are in terms of prototypes, rather than in terms of necessary-and-sufficient conditions. The most prototypical value of P_4 is indeed 'day before yesterday (or a few days earlier)', while the prototypical value of P_5 is indeed 'a year or more ago'; but the intervening period can be referred to by either of these tenses, in non-prototypical use, depending on the subjective remoteness that the speaker wants to assign to the situation referred to.

1.7 Meaning and implicature

One of the major advances in recent semantic theory has been the recognition of the distinction between the meaning of a linguistic item, in terms of its conventionalised semantic representation, and the implicatures that can be drawn from the use of a linguistic item in a particular context.[23] Among the most famous examples is the use of *it's cold in here* as a request to get someone to close the window. The meaning clearly relates to the temperature in a given space, but in a context, such as most normal contexts, where reflections on temperature are unlikely to be directly germane to the conversation, the hearer can deduce that this sentence is not intended literally, but rather that the speaker has some ulterior motive, which by a chain of reasoning can be deduced to be the speaker's desire to have the temperature raised, for instance by closing the window.

The major test for distinguishing between what is part of the meaning of a sentence and that sentence's implicatures is that the latter, but not the former, can be cancelled. Thus, with our example *it's cold in here*, when the hearer goes to close the window, the speaker might continue *please don't*

[23] For the notion of conversational implicature, see Grice (1975), Lyons (1977: 592–596).

close the window, I enjoy the cold, without contradicting himself. If, however, he were to try to cancel the meaning of his sentence, for instance by saying *please don't close the window, it's hot in here*, then he would be contradicting himself.

Although the principled distinction between meaning and implicature is crucial to a correct semantic analysis of linguistic items, carrying out the distinction in practice is by no means easy, since it often requires the construction of subtle situations to distinguish between the meaning of a form and its implicature. No doubt many instances remain where linguistic items have been assigned as meanings that should more properly be assigned as implicatures. In the discussion of section 1.6, we mentioned some instances where there is controversy over the distribution of meaning and implicature (even where a different terminology was used in earlier discussions of this problem): for instance, one could interpret the claim that the English future is basically a mood, with specific temporal interpretations in context, as saying that the meaning of the English future is modal, but that in certain contexts this modal meaning will give rise to temporal reference interpretations. Thus, if the basic meaning of the future were to be prediction, then it would be quite natural for predictions to be typically about the future, although it would also be possible for them to be about the present (*it will be raining already*), or even about the past (*he will have left already*). In the remainder of this section, we will examine some examples where the linguist might well be misled by implicatures into giving an incorrect analysis of the meaning of a tense, but where it is possible to demonstrate that there is indeed a better analysis which avoids these pitfalls.

The English past tense refers to a situation that held at some time prior to the present moment. Often, it seems that the use of past tense forms also carries the information that the situation no longer holds, as in *John used to live in London*. If this sentence were used without any disclaimer, then it would probably be taken to carry the information that John no longer lives in London. That this is only an implicature, and not part of the meaning, can be seen from the ease with which this piece of information can be cancelled, for instance by appending *and he still does*, or *and as far as I am aware he still does* (see further section 2.2).

In comparing the English perfect, simple past, and pluperfect, as in the following sentences: *John has broken his leg, John broke his leg*, and *John had broken his leg*, one gets the impression of a steady movement backwards in time, i.e. although all three refer to a situation in the past of John's breaking his leg, the first seems to be closest to the present moment, while the last seems most remote from the present moment. However, this is not part of the meaning of these verb forms, and the apparent degrees of remoteness can easily be shown to be illusory. The perfect indicates that the past situation has current relevance (i.e. relevance at the present moment), while the simple past does not carry this element of meaning (thus one natural interpretation of the perfect in this example is that John's leg is at the moment broken).[24] It is more likely that recent events will have current relevance than more remote events, whence the tendency, out of context, to interpret the perfect as referring to a more recent event than the simple past. However, if John's leg is currently broken, then the perfect can be used no matter how long ago the break took place, as in *John has broken his leg – it happened six weeks ago, and it still hasn't healed*. English has a rule preventing occurrence of the perfect with a time adverbial referring to a specific time point in the past, so that if we want to locate John's breaking his leg in time by means of such a time adverbial, then the simple past must be used, even for referring to a very recent event, as in *John broke/*has broken his leg five minutes ago*, even though five minutes ago is much more recent than six weeks ago.

The meaning of the pluperfect (see further section 3.2) is the location of a situation prior to a reference point that is itself in the past, so that in *John had broken his leg before we arrived* a past reference point is defined by the past tense adverb *arrived*, and John's breaking his leg is located prior to this reference point. Since there is necessarily a past situation prior to some other past situation, the pluperfect does, other things being equal, receive an interpretation of greater temporal remoteness. However, it is easy to construct mini-narratives where a pluperfect in fact refers to a situation subsequent to some situation referred to in the simple past, as in *John arrived an hour ago, but he had already left again before Jane arrived*; here the pluperfect locates John's departure prior to Jane's arrival, and since Jane's arrival is subsequent to John's arrival, it is possible (and indeed the only coherent interpretation) to assume that John's arrival, expressed by the simple past, in fact antedates his departure, expressed by the pluperfect.

The separation of meaning from implicature thus enables us first to give a more accurate characterisation of the meaning of a linguistic form, and secondly, given a theory of implicatures, to account for the implicatures that are assigned to linguistic forms in the absence of any cancellation of those implicatures. Another example discussed in the body of the book is the future perfect, e.g. *John will have finished his essay by next Tuesday*, which carries an implicature of future time reference, i.e. that John's

---

[24] Cf. Leech (1971: 30–35).

finishing his essay will take place in the future, although this is not part of its meaning (section 3.2). Before leaving this problem, it should be noted that in the historical development of languages, one possible change is for an implicature to be reinterpreted as part of the meaning, or indeed as the meaning. Thus in the history of many Romance languages an original perfect, with a meaning at least similar to that of the English perfect, was reinterpreted as a recent past tense (see chapter 4). In modern Eastern Armenian, an original pluperfect has been reinterpreted as a remote past.[25] It may also be noted that speakers of West African languages with grammatical distinctions of degrees of remoteness in the past often treat the English pluperfect as a translation equivalent of their own remote past tense.[26] This does not, however, affect the synchronic claim that remoteness is not part of the meaning of the English pluperfect. Thus, it would not be possible in English to say simply, out of context, *the Romans had conquered Britain*, even though the situation referred to is indeed remote.

1.8 Tense, grammar, and discourse

In this book, the approach adopted is that tenses have meanings definable independently of particular contexts; it is possible for a given tense to have more than one meaning, in which case some of the meanings may be more basic than others; it is also possible that a tense will receive particular interpretations in particular contexts, but these are always explainable in terms of the interaction of context-independent meaning and context, and do not therefore form part of the meaning of the tense category in question. This approach may be contrasted with an alternative, much in vogue with respect to tense and, even more so, aspect, according to which these categories should be defined primarily in terms of their contextual functions.[27] In this section, we will examine in detail one particular example to which this controversy applies, namely the interpretation of sequential events assigned to perfective past verbs in a narrative; notice that the interpretation of sequence, if indeed part of the meaning of the forms in question, would mean that they should by definition be assigned to the category of tense, because sequencing is one way of locating situations in time (relative to other situations). We will argue, however, that this sequencing is an implicature, deducible from the context by general conversational principles, and not part of the meaning of these forms. We will then proceed to examine ways in which context can give insight into the

[25] Fairbanks & Stevick (1958: 243–244).
[26] Larry Hyman (personal communication).
[27] For a recent defence of this discourse-based approach, see Hopper (1982).

meaning of tense forms, in particular through collocation with time adverbials, though without compromising the basic claim that the definition of tense is independent of context.

The illustrative example for the interaction of perfective aspect, context, and sequential interpretation will be taken from Russian, since Russian has an overt perfective/imperfective distinction.[28] It should be noted that the English translation will serve equally well, once one excludes from consideration the possible habitual interpretation of the English simple past. In the Russian example, (P) is placed after each verb in the perfective aspect, while the same symbol is placed after each translation equivalent verb in the English version:

—Ja ètogo ne govoril, —zasmejalsja (P) Uzelkov. Vynul (P) iz karmana svežuju pačku papiros, razorval (P) ee s ugla, vytrjas (P) na ladon' tri papirosy. Odnu zažal (P) v zubax, dve protjanul (P) nam. Potom dostal (P) spički.
'I didn't say that,' laughed (P) Uzelkov. He took out (P) from his pocket a fresh packet of cigarettes, tore (P) it open at the corner, shook out (P) onto his palm three cigarettes. One he held (P) in his teeth, two he held out (P) to us. Then he got (P) the matches.

Clearly, the only coherent interpretation of this narrative is that the linear order of the clauses corresponds to the chronological order of the events described, i.e. one does indeed assign an interpretation of sequencing such that each event is located in time after the time location of the previously mentioned event. However, it is quite possible to make up sequences of clauses with perfective verbs where there is no necessary interpretation of chronological sequence, if, for instance, the context makes it unlikely that the speaker knows the actual sequence of events, or if the sequentiality is explicitly denied (for instance by adding *but not in that order*, or *but not necessarily in that order*).

Suppose, for instance, that someone is describing the results of a violent storm that had taken place the previous night; in such a context, it is quite likely that the speaker will not know the exact order of events, but rather is reporting the sum total of what happened, as in:[29]

V tečenie noči veter sorval (P) kryšu, razbil (P) tri okna i razrubil (P) jablonju.
During the night the wind tore off (P) the roof, broke (P) three windows and brought down (P) the apple-tree.

In fact, in this example, it is not even necessary that the three windows were all broken at the same time – it is quite possible that one was broken before the wind tore off the roof, one after the apple-tree was brought down, and

[28] This example, from Nilin's novel *Žestokost'* (*Cruelty*), is cited in this context by Forsyth (1970: 65).
[29] Cf. Comrie (1976: 5).

one between these two events. It is also possible that one single gust of wind did all of this damage simultaneously. This is a classic illustration of an interpretation which is an implicature, rather than part of the meaning of a grammatical form: in an appropriate context, the implicature is cancelled.

It still remains to show in more detail how the implicature arises in more neutral contexts. Since a perfective verb form, by definition, encodes an event globally, it is representable as a point on the time line.[30] Although it is possible for a number of events to occur absolutely simultaneously, it is relatively unlikely for such a coincidence to occur, therefore the more natural interpretation is that the events did not occur simultaneously. If the events did not occur simultaneously, then the most orderly presentation, i.e. the one adhering to Grice's maxim of manner ('be orderly'),[31] is for the chronological order of events to be reflected directly in the order of presentation, if the speaker is capable of doing so (i.e. if he knows the order of events). In a narrative, this maxim of clarity is in fact heightened by the structure of the narrative itself: a narrative is by definition an account of a sequence of chronologically ordered events (real or imaginary), and for a narrative to be well-formed it must be possible to work out the chronological order of events from the structure of the narrative with minimal difficulty; this constraint of minimal difficulty means that the easiest way to present these events is with their chronological order directly reflected in the order of presentation. It is thus the interaction of the meaning of perfective aspect, the context, and conversational principles that gives rise, in neutral contexts, to the interpretation of sequentiality for a succession of perfective verbs. Sequentiality (and more generally, time reference) is thus not part of the meaning of the perfective.

While the example of perfective aspect is an interesting theoretical illustration of the danger of mistaking implicature for meaning, it also has immense practical importance, as we shall see in chapter 3. Grammars of many languages claim that the language in question has a special form for indicating situations that occur in sequence, or for distinguishing sequences of situations from simultaneously occurring situations. However, in nearly every case, it is impossible to tell from the limited range of examples given whether the interpretation of sequentiality is indeed part of the meaning of the form in question, or whether this is just an implicature following from a basically aspectual distinction. This is one of the major deficiencies of descriptive work in this domain. More generally, the failure to distinguish between meaning and implicature is one of the main problems in working out an adequate characterisation of tenses.

[30] Comrie (1976: 3–4).　　[31] Grice (1975).

The decision not to base the analysis of tense on discourse function does not, however, mean that the study of tenses in discourse is not a relevant study, indeed it is often the case that the investigation of the meaning of a tense (or of some other grammatical category) can best be approached by studying its use in discourse: rather, all that is argued here is that the investigation of the use of a grammatical category in discourse should not be confused with the meaning of that category; instead, the discourse functions should ultimately be accounted for in terms of the interaction of meaning and context.

The importance of context as a tool in investigating meaning of tense can be seen in a number of examples, including the following concerning degrees of remoteness in past and future tense (see further chapter 4). In languages which distinguish degrees of remoteness in their tense system, it is important to ascertain what the precise boundaries between different past or future tenses are. In some instances it turns out that the boundaries are absolute, i.e. defined in terms of some boundary established relative to the present moment. Thus with the past tenses in Haya, P1 is used strictly for situations that held earlier today, and may not be used for earlier situations;[32] P2 is used strictly for situations that held yesterday, and may not be used for earlier situations or later situations; while P3 is used only for situations that held before yesterday. This can be established by observing that P2 is compatible with the adverb *nyéígolo* 'yesterday', but not with *mbwéénu* 'today' or *íjo* 'the day before yesterday': *tukomíle nyéígolo/ *mbwéénu/*íjo* 'I tied (P2) yesterday/*today/*the day before yesterday'. Even if one wants to create the impression of subjective remoteness or closeness to the present moment, the meaning of P2, which includes location in time restricted to the day before the speech event, precludes combination of P2 with an adverbial specifying time location before or after yesterday.

In other instances, however, the boundaries for tenses separated by degrees of remoteness are more fluid, so that choice of an atypical tense for a given objective degree of remoteness is possible, in order to give a subjective impression of closeness to or remoteness from the present moment. In Haya, this fluid boundary characterises the division between the two future tenses. Although the basic distinction is that F1 is used for situations holding later on today or tomorrow, while F2 is used for events holding later than tomorrow, it is possible to combine F1 with a time adverbial of more distant time reference to create the subjective impression of imminence, e.g. *mwézy' ógulaijá tu-laa-gy-á Katoke* 'month coming we-go (F1)

[32] The Haya material is from unpublished work by Ernest R. Byarushengo.

Katoke', i.e. 'next month we will go to Katoke'. Use of the F2 tense *tu-li-gy-á* would also be possible with the same truth-functional meaning, but without the subjective impression of imminence. (In Haya it is, however, impossible to use F2 with reference to a situation holding later on today or tomorrow; thus, with *nyenkyá* 'tomorrow', we have *nyenkyá tu-laa-gy-á* (F1)/*tu-li-gy-á* (F2) *Katoke* 'tomorrow we will go to Katoke'.)

Although collocation of tenses with time adverbials can be an important tool in investigating the meaning of tenses, it should again be emphasised that this tool cannot be applied mechanically, since the intervention of other factors may upset any simple correlation between tense and time adverbial. An English example may serve as an illustration of the complex relation that may obtain between a time adverbial and location in time. At first sight, it would seem that an adverbial like *at six o'clock* would necessarily define the location in time of the situation referred to by the rest of the sentence. However, the example *the prime minister will make a speech at six o'clock* demonstrates that this straightforward correlation does not hold invariably. The rest of this sentence refers to the situation of the prime minister's making a speech, but given that speeches are not instantaneous events, the normal interpretation given to this sentence is that the time adverbial refers to the beginning of the speech, i.e. in English it is sometimes possible to collocate punctual time adverbials with durative situations in order to give the time point of the beginning of the durative situation. But note that the rest of the sentence does not refer to the beginning of the durative situation, and there is in fact a subtle difference between *the prime minister will make a speech at six o'clock* and *the prime minister will begin to make a speech at six o'clock*, which becomes perhaps clearer if the sentences are put into the past tense. Imagine a situation where the prime minister did indeed begin the speech at six o'clock, but was then arrested one minute later by the ringleaders of a coup d'état and prevented from completing the speech. It would be perfectly natural to report this as *the prime minister began to make a speech at six o'clock, but was prevented from making the speech by the rebels*, but very strange to report this as *the prime minister made a speech at six o'clock, but was prevented from making the speech by the rebels*. In particular, although the time adverbial *six o'clock* refers to the time of the beginning of the speech in *the prime minister made a speech at six o'clock* the situation described by the rest of the sentence is the whole of the prime minister's speech, which thus leads to self-contradiction if we go on to say that the prime minister did not make a whole speech.

Another example illustrating the problems that obtain in correlating tense with time adverbials comes from languages where tense is normally not marked when there is lexical specification of the time location of a situation. In Mam, tense is indicated by sentence-initial particles, in particular *ma* 'recent past' and *o* 'past', e.g. *ma chin jaw tz' aq-a* 'recent:past I up slip I :singular', i.e. 'I slipped (just now)', *o chin jaw tz'aq-a* 'I slipped a while ago'. If, however, an overt adverbial of time occurs sentence-initially, then the tense particle is obligatorily omitted, e.g. *eew tz-ul aaj nan yaa7* 'yesterday he/she hither return ma'am grandmother', i.e. 'grandmother came yesterday'; it is not possible to have both *eew* and *o*. The same is true in the recent past: *maaky' ø-jaw we7* 'a :while :ago he up stand', i.e. 'he got up a little while ago', where it is impossible to insert *ma*.[33] A similar, though less strict collocation restriction is found in many Creoles. In Jamaican Creole, for instance, it is usual to omit tense markers when an overt adverbial of time location is present: compare *mi en a sing* 'I anterior progressive sing', i.e. 'I was singing', with *yeside mi (?en) a sing* 'yesterday I was singing'. Such virtual complementary distribution between tense and time adverbial means collocation cannot be used as a test for time location values in tenses.

When one takes into account the interaction of tense with other facets of the syntax of a language (see further chapter 5), one can find a wide range of examples where there is apparent conflict between the time reference of a tense and a co-occurring adverbial. Thus in Portuguese, the simple past normally has past time reference, and this forms part of its meaning. However, it is possible to have sentences like *quando você chegar, eu já saí* 'when you arrive, I will already have left', where the verb in the second clause is in the simple past, although it is interpreted as having future time reference (cf. the future perfect in the English translation). This can be accounted for by a general rule of Portuguese, especially spoken Portuguese, whereby future time reference is expressed by the present tense, and correspondingly time reference that is anterior to some future reference point (expected tense equivalent: future perfect) is replaced by a form normally indicating time reference that is anterior to the present moment, i.e. the simple past. The same explanation governs the possible uses of the perfect in German in sentences like *bis morgen bin ich schon weggefahren* 'by tomorrow I will already have departed', literally '. . . I have already departed'. In indirect speech in English, where the tense of verbs is determined by a combination of the tense used in the original direct speech and a rule of sequence of tenses putting verbs into a past tense after a main verb in the past, it is possible (at least for some speakers) to get such apparent conflicts of tense and adverbial time reference as *by next week*

[33] The Mam data are from England (1983: 161–164, 191–192, 284–286).

John will be claiming that he arrived tomorrow, as a way of reporting John's (predicted) actual words 'I arrived on Tuesday', assuming that the report is made on Monday (see further section 5.3). What is crucial is that all such apparent counter-examples to the meaning of tense forms can be given a principled account in terms of the basic meaning of the tense in question and independently justified syntactic principles that interact with this basic meaning.

A particularly complex instance of the interaction of temporal location reference and time adverbial is provided by the English perfect. Since I would claim that the English perfect is not to be analysed simply as a tense, in particular that it differs from other English past tenses in terms of parameters other than tense, the perfect will not be analysed in detail in this book, but some indication will nonetheless be given of the problems that arise if one tries to establish the time reference of the perfect by means of collocation with time adverbials. Most recent analyses of the perfect agree that the difference between perfect and (other) past tenses is that the former carries an added semantic component of present relevance, i.e. *John has broken his leg* indicates that the past situation of John's breaking his leg still has present relevance.[34]

In general, the perfect is incompatible with time adverbials that have definite past time reference, i.e. time adverbials that refer to a specific moment or stretch of time located wholly in the past. Thus English excludes sentences like **John has broken his leg yesterday*, and this constraint crucially overrides even considerations of present relevance. This might lead one to the conclusion that the perfect is not a past tense. However, there are problems with this conclusion, apart from the general caveat discussed above of mechanically applying collocation with time adverbials as a test for time location reference of tenses.

The first, and least significant, objection is that several other languages have a perfect with more or less the same range of functions as the English perfect, but nonetheless without the restriction against collocation with time adverbials of past time reference, cf. Norwegian *jeg har sett ham for et øyeblikk siden* 'I saw [literally: have seen] him a moment ago', *i natt har jeg sovet godt* 'last night I slept [literally: have slept] well'.[35] This might simply mean that the meaning of the perfect in English is different from that of the perfect in these other languages, whence naturally one might expect different collocation possibilities with time adverbials. It should, however, be noted that the particular restriction found in English is cross-linguistically unusual for a grammatical category, and one might wonder

[34] See, for instance, Comrie (1976: 52–61).   [35] Vannebo (1979: 213).

whether this particular restriction in English should play so fundamental a role in so many attempts at building up general theories of tense.

The second objection is that, with considerable dialectal and idiolectal variation, some speakers of English do allow time adverbials referring to specific points or periods of time in the past to co-occur with the perfect. All speakers allow collocation with the adverbial *recently*, e.g. *I have recently met an interesting poet*, even though the time reference of *recently* is wholly in the past, albeit continuing up until infinitesimally before the present moment; *recently* is, of course, incompatible with the present tense, so that it would be contradictory to argue that the perfect is a present tense on the grounds that it cannot occur with past time adverbials (and can occur with some present time adverbials – see below), while disregarding the evidence that it can co-occur with *recently*. Some speakers also allow collocation of the perfect with time adverbials locating the situation in a time segment in the very recent past, for example earlier on the day in which the speech situation takes place, e.g. *I have seen him this morning*, said during the afternoon (i.e. when *this morning* refers to a time period in the past).[36] There is also at least one idiom referring to the distant past where the perfect is allowed, namely with *long since*, as in *I have long since given up drinking*, where the adverbial *long since* clearly points to a very remote situation of giving up drinking, albeit with currently continuing results.[37]

Just as the (alleged) non-collocation with past time adverbials would seem to be an argument against assigning past time reference to the English perfect, the possibility of collocating this form with present time adverbials might seem to be an argument in favour of assigning it present time reference. However, the circumstances under which the perfect is felicitously collocated with a time adverbial of present time reference are remarkably restricted. The most natural uses of the perfect are in fact where the time reference of the sentence incorporates both the present moment and the time of the previous situation referred to in the sentence which has continuing current relevance.[38] Thus, in the sentence *I have seen him today*, the time adverbial *today* includes both the present moment and the point of time at which I saw him. The most natural interpretation for a sentence like *I have collected ten signatures today* is that today incorporates both the present moment (of course) and also the time period during which I gathered those ten signatures, i.e. all of the signatures were collected today.

[36] Leech (1971: 41).
[37] I am grateful to R. van Oirsouw for this observation.
[38] This discussion is an expanded version of Comrie (1981).

Interpretations in which the time reference of the adverbial includes the present moment but not the past situations that have current relevance are usually more forced, requiring the presence of either specific lexical items or of contextual features that force this interpretation. The lexical item *now* readily occurs with this interpretation, as in *I have now collected ten signatures*, where *now* receives the interpretation *up to now*, although the adverbial itself strictly includes only the present moment, and not the time during which the signatures were collected. However, use of adverbials which are coreferential with *now* requires specific circumstances for their use, as in *at six o'clock I have collected ten signatures*, which suggests someone looking at his watch at six o'clock, and simply using the adverbial *at six o'clock* as a more accurately recordable alternative to *now*.

Where the past situation that has current relevance is cumulative, as with gathering signatures, the most natural interpretation, as noted above, seems to be that the past situation as well as the present moment are included within the time adverbial, as in the interpretation suggested above for *I have collected ten signatures today*. There is, however, a possible alternative interpretation, according to which ten is the cumulative number of signatures I have gathered up to and including today, although some, indeed all, of the signatures might have been gathered before today. This interpretation becomes more salient if the context makes it unlikely that the whole of the accumulation took place in one day, as in *I have collected ten million signatures today*, perhaps more natural if the adverbial is preposed to give *today, I have collected ten million signatures*, although the use of an expression like *up to today* or *so far* still seems much more natural, i.e. a time adverbial which explicitly incorporates the time during which the collection took place as well as the present moment.

Where the past situation is non-cumulative, then use of a time adverbial with present time reference is highly dubious. Thus if in fact I met John in 1970, and have not met him since, it would not be possible to say *I have met John today*, although it would of course be possible to say *I have met John*. Yet the claim that the perfect has present time reference because of its collocability with present time adverbials would claim that *I have met John today* should have the interpretation just outlined, since the time adverbial includes the present moment. Such examples suggest strongly, therefore, that the time of the past situation is also relevant to the establishment of collocation restrictions on time adverbials occurring with the perfect in English.

The above discussion has not attempted to solve the problem of the time reference of the English perfect, and since factors going beyond time reference are involved (e.g. continuing relevance) we shall not pursue this topic any further here, other than perhaps to note that an adequate solution will probably have to combine past and present time reference. The discussion has, however, served to indicate how complex the interaction can be between the time location part of the meaning of a grammatical form and the time adverbials with which it can co-occur, and to warn against the simplistic application of collocation tests in trying to establish the meaning of tenses.

All of this should not be taken to deny that there are certain verb forms in some languages whose basic meaning includes a component of discourse. In French, for instance, the simple past is used only in (written) narrative, where it encodes events in the past (or at least, which are presented as being in the past). However, the discourse part of the meaning of this grammatical category is not one of tense. This point is not purely terminological, although it might seem to be so given our definition of tense as the grammaticalisation of location in time, which thus automatically excludes such discourse factors. Rather, the claim is an existence claim: that there do exist grammatical categories cross-linguistically which encode (as at least part of their basic meaning) location in time, and that this set of grammatical categories is sufficiently coherent cross-linguistically to justify the establishment of a general linguistic category of tense defined in this way. To attempt a broader definition would in fact destroy the homogeneity of the concept and therefore the possibility of a general theory of tense.

2
Absolute tense

The term absolute tense is a traditional, though somewhat misleading term, that has come to be used to refer to tenses which take the present moment as their deictic centre. The term is misleading because, strictly speaking, absolute time reference is impossible, since the only way of locating a situation in time is relative to some other already established time point; the present moment is in principle just one of an infinite number of such time points that could be chosen as reference point, although it does play a major role in the definition of tense systems across the languages of the world. There is thus a real sense in which taking the present moment as the deictic centre establishes the most basic tenses cross-linguistically, those in terms of which it is often easier to understand deviations from absolute tense. We shall continue to use the traditional term absolute tense, although it should be borne in mind that this should be interpreted to mean a tense which includes as part of its meaning the present moment as deictic centre; whereas relative tense (chapter 3) refers to a tense which does not include as part of its meaning the present moment as deictic centre.

Given the present moment as deictic centre, it might seem trivial to define the three basic tenses that have formed the backbone of much linguistic work on time reference in grammar, namely present, past and future, as follows: present tense means coincidence of the time of the situation and the present moment; past tense means location of the situation prior to the present moment; future tense means location of the situation after the present moment. The body of this chapter will be devoted to demonstrating that, while these characterisations are basically correct, it is essential to amplify them somewhat to ensure a correct characterisation of these three absolute tenses.

2.1 Present tense

The time line diagram introduced in section 1.2 identifies the present moment as a point in time on that line, and the basic meaning of present tense is thus location of a situation at that point.

36

However, it is relatively rare for a situation to coincide exactly with the present moment, i.e. to occupy, literally or in terms of our conception of the situation, a single point in time which is exactly commensurate with the present moment. Situations of this rare type do, however, occur, and of course the present tense is an appropriate form to use in locating them temporally. One set of examples falling under this rubric would be performative sentences, i.e. sentences where the act described by the sentence is performed by uttering the sentence in question, e.g. *I promise to pay you ten pounds* (utterance of this sentence constitutes the promise to pay ten pounds), *I name this ship the 'Titanic'* (utterance of this sentence, under the appropriate circumstances, constitutes the act of naming the ship).[1] Although these situations are not strictly momentaneous, since it takes a certain period of time to utter even the shortest sentence, they can be conceptualised as momentaneous, especially in so far as the time occupied by the report is exactly the same as the time occupied by the act, i.e. at each point in the utterance of the sentence there is coincidence between the present moment with regard to the utterance and the present moment with regard to the act in question.

Another set of examples where there is literal coincidence between the time location of a situation and the present moment is with simultaneous reports of an ongoing series of events. Thus when a horse-racing commentator says *Red Rover crosses the finishing line*, his utterance of this sentence coincides, or at least is taken conceptually to coincide, with the event of Red Rover's crossing the finishing line; and since the report is simultaneous with the situation being described, there is literal location of a situation at the present moment in time. However, situations of the kinds described are relatively rare, and the more normal uses of the present tense, in languages where this is a separate grammatical category, go far beyond this restricted range. It will therefore be necessary to discuss further examples in order to refine the definition of the present tense, and our interpretation of this definition.

A more characteristic use of the present tense is in referring to situations which occupy a much longer period of time than the present moment, but which nonetheless include the present moment within them. In particular, the present tense is used to speak of states and processes which hold at the present moment, but which began before the present moment and may well continue beyond the present moment, as in *the Eiffel Tower stands in Paris* and *the author is working on chapter two*. In each of these examples, it is indeed true that the situation holds at the present moment, i.e. at this

[1] For the term 'performative', see Austin (1962).

moment the Eiffel Tower does stand in Paris, at this moment the author is indeed working on chapter two, but it is not the case that the situation is restricted only to the present moment. We must therefore ask whether the existence of such examples requires us to modify the definition of the present tense.

The claim of this book will be that it is in fact not necessary to modify the definition. As far as the present tense is concerned, in its basic meaning it invariably locates a situation at the present moment, and says nothing beyond that. In particular, it does not say that the same situation does not continue beyond the present moment, nor that it did not hold in the past. More accurately, the situation referred to by the verb in the present tense is simply a situation holding literally at the present moment; whether or not this situation is part of a larger situation extending into the past or the future is an implicature, rather than part of the meaning of the present tense, an implicature that is worked out on the basis of other features of the structure of the sentence and one's knowledge of the real world. Of other relevant features of sentence structure, aspect will be one of the most important in deciding whether the larger situation is restricted just to the present moment or not: thus, use of the progressive aspect necessarily requires that the situation in question be not momentaneous, so that use of this grammatical form will lead inevitably to an interpretation where the present moment is just one moment among many at which the larger situation holds – but this follows automatically from the meaning of the progressive, and does not compromise the meaning of the present tense. In other examples, it will be our real-world knowledge that enables us to decide whether a situation is literally to be located just at the present moment or over a period encompassing the present moment. Since Russian lacks a progressive/non-progressive aspectual distinction, the Russian translation of *the author is working on chapter two*, i.e. *avtor rabotaet nad vtoroj glavoj*, does not specify grammatically whether the situation is punctual or extended, but our knowledge of the world, in which work on a chapter of a book requires a considerable span of time, leads to the interpretation that the present moment is located within the larger situation of working on chapter two, rather than exhausting this larger situation.

Our crucial claim is thus that the present tense refers only to a situation holding at the present moment, even where that situation is part of a larger situation that occupies more than just the present moment. It is possible that other time adverbials may express the duration of the larger situation, as in *the author is working on chapter two from six o'clock until twelve o'clock today*, but it does not compromise the definition of present tense given above, rather it indicates that it is misleading to use collocation with time adverbials as a mechanical test for establishing the meaning of tenses (see section 1.8).

In many languages, the present tense is also used with habitual aspectual meaning, as in English *John goes to work at eight o'clock (every day)*. This might seem to be a clear contradiction to our definition of the present tense, since we can use this sentence to describe John's behaviour by uttering the sentence at midday, when it is clearly not literally true that John is going to work at the moment at which the sentence is uttered. This has given rise, in some accounts of tense (especially of tense in individual languages), to the setting up of separate tense categories to refer to situations that actually hold at the present moment (such as *the Eiffel Tower stands in Paris, the author is working on chapter two*) versus situations that do occur habitually but do not actually hold at the present moment, as in the example introduced in this paragraph. However, this distinction is not necessary. Sentences with habitual aspectual meaning refer not to a sequence of situations recurring at intervals, but rather to a habit, a characteristic situation that holds at all times. Thus, in our example *John goes to work at eight o'clock every day*, a certain property (namely, going to work at eight o'clock every day) is assigned to John, and this property is of course true of John even if at the moment he happens not to be on his way to work. In other words, the habit does hold at the present moment, and that is why the present tense is in principle an appropriate tense to use in describing this habitual situation.

Of course, it is quite possible that a language might have some special form other than the present tense for describing such habitual situations. In Dyirbal, for instance, there are two basic finite forms of verbs.[2] One is used for actual situations, i.e. situations that can be identified as happening at the present or having happened in the past; the other is used for situations that are not subsumed by the first form, i.e. situations that are predicted for the future, and situations that are induced to be general even though they are not observable as ongoing at the present moment or as having occurred in the past. In Dyirbal, then, this second form would be used for habitual statements. However, despite the terminology adopted for Dyirbal, which identifies the two tenses as present-past and future respectively, the distinction between them is more accurately described as one of mood, namely realis versus irrealis respectively. The realis is used for situations

---

[2] Dixon (1972: 55). Although Dixon uses the terms unmarked tense 'referring to past or present time' and future tense 'for referring to future time', his discussion makes clear that the distinction is not one of time reference, since the so-called future 'can also carry a generic meaning'.

that are ongoing or were observed in the past, the irrealis for all other situations, including situations that are presented as inductive generalisations from past observations to statements of general habit. Dyirbal therefore does not contradict the account given above of present tense, since one can say that Dyirbal has no tense distinction, and the distribution of these moods is thus irrelevant to the account of tense: interpretations of location in time are implicatures of the Dyirbal modal distinction, but not part of the meaning of this opposition.[3]

More generally, habitual meaning lies on the boundary of the three systems of tense, aspect, and mood. In principle, one could expect habituality to be expressed by means of a tense, since it involves location of a situation across a large slice of time (perhaps across the whole of time) rather than just at some single point. Habituality can also be aspectual, in that it refers to the internal temporal contour of a situation, in particular in that the situation must occupy a large slice of time. Habituality can also be modal, since it involves induction from limited observations about the actual world to a generalisation about possible worlds. Our claim, however, is that no language will indicate habituality by means of a tense opposition, and indeed the representations established in chapter 6 will not permit a tense system to make such a distinction. In part, this is definitional, a decision not to call habituality a tense, but there is also empirical content to the claim, namely that grammatical expression of habituality will always be integrated into the aspectual or modal system of a language rather than into its tense system.

Just as we claim there can be no separate habitual tense, distinct from the present, likewise we are led to claim there can be no universal tense, i.e. a tense that is used for truths that hold at all time. Thus, a sentence like *cows eat grass* is claimed to refer only to the present moment, the interpretation of this as a universal truth being on the basis of structural and extra-linguistic factors beyond the meaning of the present tense. The universality can, of course, be made explicit by a time adverbial, as in *cows always/ usually eat grass*, but this does not impinge on the meaning of the present tense. Some languages are claimed to have a universal tense, for instance Swahili, which is traditionally described as having a *na*-present tense (for ongoing situations), an *a*-universal tense (for general truths not restricted temporally), and a *hu*-habitual tense (for customarily recurring situa-

[3] Actually, this suggests that the meanings of verbs as lexical items are slightly, but systematically, different in Dyirbal and in, for instance, English. The meaning of the English verb *hit* subsumes the interpretation of propensity to hit, while its Dyirbal translation *balgal-* excludes this interpretation, whence reference to the propensity to hit in Dyirbal requires an irrealis form of the lexical item.

tions).[4] However, there is no reason for treating this as a distinction in tense rather than in aspect or mood; moreover, detailed investigation of the use of the three forms suggests that much more is involved than just the simple distinction given in elementary grammars, with pragmatic factors in particular playing an important role in the choice of tense.[5]

2.2 Past tense

Referring again to the time line as presented in section 1.2, with the present moment marked as a point on it, past tense locates a situation to the left of that present moment time point. The meaning of the past tense is thus location in time prior to the present moment, and any further deductions about temporal location that are made on the basis of individual sentences in the past tense are the result of factors other than simply the choice of tense.

Note that the past tense simply locates the situation in question prior to the present moment, and says nothing about whether the past situation occupies just a single point prior to the present moment, or an extended time period prior to the present moment, or indeed the whole of time up to the present moment, as in the following examples: *at seven o'clock yesterday John promised to give me ten pounds; John lived in Manchester from 1962 to 1982; up to this moment this disease was incurable.* Likewise, the concept past time reference is neutral as between the interpretations assigned to the following two English sentences: *John was in Paris; John has been in Paris.* The first implies the existence of a specific occasion on which John was in Paris, the ability to refer to which is shared by speaker and hearer; and of course allows that at other times in the past John need not have been in Paris; the second simply indicates that there is some time in the past, not necessarily further identifiable by speaker or hearer, at which the proposition *John be in Paris* held.[6] All of these particular interpretations are compatible with the meaning given for the past tense.

It should also be noted that use of the past tense only locates the situation in the past, without saying anything about whether that situation continues to the present or into the future, although there is often a conversational implicature that it does not continue to or beyond the present. This last point follows from Grice's maxim of relation (relevance),[7] in that, other things being equal, statements about the present moment are more relevant

---

4 Ashton (1947: 37–39).
5 I am grateful to Benji Wald for discussion on this question.
6 For discussion of the difference between perfect and simple past in English, see, for instance, Comrie (1976: 52–61), McCoard (1978).
7 Grice (1975).

than those about other times, so that use of a form explicitly locating a situation in the past suggests that that situation does not hold at the present, otherwise the present tense would be used. One example of this kind was introduced in section 1.7, namely *John used to live in London*. Here, other things being equal, an implicature will be derived that John no longer lives in London. However, it is quite possible for the rest of the context to cancel this implicature. For instance, let us suppose that it has been established that John currently lives in London. Then in reply to the question *where did he live ten years ago?*, it would be possible to reply *he used to live in London then as well*, where the context clearly indicates that the implicature 'no longer true at the present moment' is not to be derived. In this example the implicature is actually negated by the context. It is also possible for the context to leave open whether or not the implicature is true. Thus, in answer to the question *does John live in London?*, one might answer *he used to, but I don't know if he still does*, leaving it open whether or not he still lives in London.

A similar phenomenon can be seen with past progressive constructions. Thus English *John was eating his lunch (when I looked into his room)* states that at a certain period of time in the past (namely, in this example, the time point identified as when I looked into John's room), the proposition *John be eating his lunch* was true. It says nothing about whether the situation still continues at the present moment or not. Any implicature of present non-relevance can easily be cancelled contextually, so that if someone asks me whether John is eating his lunch at the moment, I can reply *he was eating his lunch five minutes ago when I looked into his room, but he may have finished by now*.

It is also possible that other features of the sentence will indicate that the situation referred to did indeed terminate in the past, but again this is because of these other features, and not because of the meaning of the past tense. In Russian, for instance, the perfective past will necessarily indicate that the situation in question was completed, since use of perfective aspect and past tense locates the whole of the situation in past time, e.g. *Kolja pročital ètu knigu* 'Kolya has read this book'.[8] Of course, at best this indicates that the situation of Kolya's reading the book referred to has terminated; this Russian sentence is not incompatible with Kolya's re-reading the book at the present moment, i.e. from *Kolja pročital ètu knigu* one cannot logically deduce that the proposition *Kolya be reading this book* is untrue at the present moment.

The question may therefore arise as to whether a language can have a

[8] See, for instance, Comrie (1976: 3–4).

grammatical form that encodes a situation which held in the past but does not hold in the present. Clearly this meaning can be expressed non-grammatically, for instance by coordinating two separate clauses (*John was reading this book five minutes ago but he is not reading it now*), or by use of the lexical item *no longer* (*John is no longer reading this book*), which carries a presupposition that he was reading the book in the past and a statement that he is not doing so at the moment. In section 2.6 we will see that indeed some languages do have tenses with this meaning, although such tenses are extremely rare across the languages of the world. The implications of this for general tense theory will be discussed in sections 2.6 and 6.5.

2.3 Future tense

In terms of the analysis of tense presented so far, it might seem straightforward to define future tense as locating a situation at a time subsequent to the present moment, i.e. to the right of the present moment on the diagram of the time line presented in section 1.2. One would then be able to elaborate on this in precisely the same way as was done for the past tense, in particular demonstrating that any deduction that the situation in question does not hold at the present moment is at best an implicature, rather than part of the meaning of the future tense. Thus *John will be eating his lunch when you call on him in five minutes' time* does not exclude the possibility that he may already have started eating his lunch. However, in the light of the great controversy that has surrounded the concept of future tense, both in general linguistic theory and in the analysis of individual languages (including English), it is necessary to examine a number of phenomena before returning to this characterisation. We will in fact conclude that this characterisation of the meaning of the future tense is correct, but the controversy surrounds not so much the definition of future tense as whether such a category is justified in linguistic theory in the first place, as a tense.

One of the objections raised to the notion of future tense is a conceptual objection. The time line diagram proposed in section 1.2 is symmetrical about the axis of the present moment, i.e. the future is presented as being essentially the same as the past, only in the opposite temporal direction. However, there is a sense in which the future is clearly different from the past. The past subsumes what may already have taken place and, barring science fiction, is immutable, beyond the control of our present actions. The future, however, is necessarily more speculative, in that any prediction we make about the future might be changed by intervening events, including our own conscious intervention. Thus, in a very real sense the past is more definite than the future. Following on from this, one might argue that while the difference between past and present is indeed one of tense, that between future on the one hand and past and present on the other should be treated as a difference of mood rather than one of tense.[9]

Notice that this conceptual objection simply says that the past and future differ from one another in certain respects. It is not inconsistent with their being similar to one another in other respects, perhaps even those crucial respects that are relevant to tense. Therefore, the question of whether future time reference is subsumed under tense or mood, whether in general linguistic theory or in some specific language, is an empirical question that can only be answered on the basis of the investigation of grammatical expressions of future time reference across a number of languages. This task will be adumbrated in the following paragraphs. For the moment, however, it should be noted that the so-called future tense in English makes a clear prediction about some future state of affairs, and is in this way clearly distinct from modal constructions that make reference to alternative worlds.[10] Thus *it will rain tomorrow* is a very definite statement about a state of affairs to hold at a certain time subsequent to the present moment, and its truth can be tested at that future time by seeing whether it does in fact rain or not. This can be contrasted with *it may rain tomorrow*, which is simply a claim about a possible world in which there is rain tomorrow; the truth value of this statement cannot be assessed by observing whether or not it rains tomorrow (since both presence and absence of rain are compatible with *may rain*) – indeed, evaluation of the truth of such a modal statement is extremely difficult, involving demonstrating the existence or non-existence of a certain possible world which may not coincide with the actual world. It is thus possible to have future time reference which is not necessarily modal.

Another relevant observation that might constitute an objection to the symmetrical conceptualisation of time is that many languages, including most European languages, have a clear grammatical distinction between past and non-past (the latter subsuming present and future time reference), but either no grammatical distinction or a much less clear grammatical distinction between future and non-future, in particular between future and present. In many European languages, the so-called present tense is in fact the normal verb form used to indicate future time reference, as for instance in German *ich gehe morgen* or Finnish *minä menen huomenna* 'I will go [literally: I go] tomorrow'. These languages do also have specific construc-

---

[9] For a recent study of the interaction between future time reference and mood, with particular reference to the Romance languages, see Fleischman (1982).

[10] Compare the discussion in McCawley (1981: 342–343).

tions with exclusively future time reference, e.g. German *ich werde gehen*, Finnish *minä tulen menemään* or *minä olen menevä* 'I will go', but such constructions are normally only used where there would otherwise be danger of misunderstanding in the direction of present time reference, especially in Finnish, where the so-called present tense is by far the most usual form to express future as well as present time reference. In these languages, then, one might say that the only tenses distinguished grammatically are past and non-past (see section 2.4). What this would demonstrate is that these languages lack a future tense, but this would not in itself be proof that the concept of future tense is not needed in general linguistic theory: since the general theory must be able to deal with the tense system of any language, it would be necessary to show that no language has a grammaticalised future tense.

The converse of the above observation is that a number of languages do not allow use of the same form for expressing present and future time reference. This might seem to establish future tense as a separate grammatical category for such languages. This is not, however, necessarily the case. In many such instances, the use of a distinct form for present and for future time reference is not due to the tense system of the language in question, but rather to its modal system. As we saw in section 2.1, some languages have a basic modal distinction between realis and irrealis, where realis refers to situations that have actually taken place or are actually taking place, while irrealis is used for more hypothetical situations, including situations that represent inductive generalisations, and also predictions, including also predictions about the future. We mentioned Dyirbal as one language of this kind. Another example is Burmese, where the sentence-final particle *-te/ thǎ/ta/hta* is used for realis while the sentence-final particle *-me/mǎ/hma* is used for irrealis (see further section 2.4).[11] Since future time reference in these languages is subsumed under irrealis, while present time reference (in the absence of any other modal value) is subsumed under realis, it is indeed the case that present and future time reference will have different grammatical realisations, but without it being the case that these languages have a distinct future tense. Rather, future time reference is just one of the interpretations possible for the irrealis, and there is no reason to assume that it is significantly more basic than any of the other interpretations of this form.

Finally, one might observe that expressions of future time reference frequently derive diachronically from modal expressions, e.g. of desiderativity, such as English *will*. However, this diachronic relation says

[11] Okell (1969: 173, 354–357, 424–428).

nothing of the synchronic status of such forms. Further historical development may even separate them formally, as has happened in Chukchi: the
prefix *re-/ra-* together with the suffix *-ŋ* indicates either desiderative mood
or future tense, but several desiderative and future forms are now distinct,
for instance, in that the aspectual suffix *-rkə(n(i))-* follows modal *-ŋ* but
precedes temporal *-ŋ*, e.g. *re-nike-rkəni-ŋ-ət* 'they will do likewise',
re-nike-ŋə-rk-ət 'they want to do likewise'.

We are therefore left with the problem of finding a language in which
there is a separate grammatical form used for future time reference, but
where the use of this form cannot be treated as a special use of a grammatical
category with basically non-tense meaning. This considerably reduces the
number of candidates for future tense, and moreover requires a sophisti-
cated analysis of the languages that are advanced as candidates, since a
superficial examination will not reveal whether or not a given expression of
future time reference is in fact a distinct tense or just a form with more
general meaning subsuming future time reference. Nonetheless, there are
some languages which appear from the literature to illustrate the existence
of clear-cut future tenses. In languages which distinguish different degrees
of remoteness in the future, i.e. have near and distant futures, especially if
there are several degrees of remoteness distinguished, it appears that at least
most of the relevant categories can only be used specifically with future time
reference, i.e. they are future tenses (for the material, see chapter 4). Thus
in Haya, the remote future tense can only be used in referring to a situation
which is located temporally subsequent to tomorrow, and collocation with
any other time reference (e.g. past, present time reference, or reference to
tomorrow) is ungrammatical on any interpretation.[12] In addition, there are
some languages lacking degrees of remoteness in the future but where
nonetheless there is a specific future tense which does not have modal uses
with non-future time reference in addition to its temporal use: such is the
case with the future tense in Hua, a language with a basic tense distinction
between future and non-future (section 2.5).[13]

Some further discussion of the English system is appropriate at this
point. Traditional grammar usually presents English as having a future
tense, namely the form using the auxiliary *will* (for some speakers, also
shall) and the citation form of the verb, as in *John will leave tomorrow*.
There are two directions in which one could object to this analysis. First,
the auxiliary *will* has a number of other uses in addition to the expression of
future time reference, in particular modal uses which do not necessarily

[12] Information on Haya is from Ernest R. Byarushengo.
[13] Haiman (1980: 140–144).

have future time reference:[14] in particular, *will* can be used to indicate volition with present time reference (*he will go swimming in dangerous waters*), and prediction with present time reference might well be subsumed under the latter of these modal uses, in particular. From the other direction, there are many instances of future time reference where it is not necessary to use the auxiliary *will*, but where rather the so-called present tense suffices, as in *the train departs at five o'clock tomorrow morning*. Thus future time reference is neither a necessary nor a sufficient condition for the use of *will* in English.

Before abandoning the claim that English has a future tense, however, it is necessary to ask the question whether the correlation between *will* and future time reference in English is explainable in its entirety in terms independent of future time reference, or whether future time reference will still have to play some explicit role in determining the circumstances under which *will* can be used or omitted. It is remarkable that, for a language as thoroughly investigated as English, this question remains unanswered. We will suggest that there is indeed need to refer independently to future time reference, but it is of course possible that subsequent work may lead to revision of this claim, by showing that these instances of apparent relevance of future time reference can in fact be subsumed under some more general non-tense category.

In main clauses, there is a heavy constraint on the use of the present tense with future time reference, namely that the situation referred to must be one that is scheduled. In our example above, *the train departs at five o'clock tomorrow morning*, use of the present tense is justified because the situation referred to is indeed one that is scheduled.[15] However, the sentence *it rains tomorrow* is decidedly odd, indeed on asking a naive native speaker of English one would probably receive the reaction that the sentence is unacceptable. The reason why the sentence is odd is that it requires an interpretation under which the occurrence of rain tomorrow is scheduled, and our knowledge of the world as it is today indicates that rain is not schedulable in this way. The sentence would, however, be acceptable, if

---

[14] See, for instance, the discussion in Leech (1971: 77–80).

[15] Note that the sentence *the train departs at five o'clock tomorrow morning* is not claimed to have the same meaning as *the train is scheduled to depart at five o'clock tomorrow morning*; the former does say explicitly that the train will depart at the said hour, and moreover that this is the result of scheduling; the latter, however, says only that according to the schedule five o'clock is the train's departure time, but does not say that the train will in fact leave according to that schedule. It is thus perfectly reasonable to say *the train is scheduled to leave at five o'clock tomorrow morning, but in fact it won't leave till six*, while it would be a self-contradiction to say *the train departs at five o'clock tomorrow morning, but in fact it won't leave till six*.

one imagined a context where rain is schedulable, e.g. if God is talking, or if advances in meteorology made it possible for humans to schedule rain. This suggests that, in accounting for the use of the construction with *will*, it will be necessary to make explicit separate reference to scheduling and to future time reference.

In some subordinate clauses, in particular in temporal and conditional clauses, the auxiliary *will* with future time reference is normally excluded, even in instances where in main clauses *will* would be required because of absence of scheduling.[16] Thus alongside *it will rain tomorrow*, we have *if it *will rain/rains tomorrow, we will get wet*. In conditional clauses, *will* with modal meaning is permitted, e.g. *if he will go swimming in dangerous waters, he will drown*. Thus future time reference uses of *will* are grammatically distinct from modal uses of *will* in such subordinate clauses, so that again the grammar will have to refer directly to the feature of future time reference. These examples therefore suggest (but do not, of course, prove) that English does have a separate grammatical category of future time reference, i.e. a future tense.

On the basis of the discussion in this section, we will assume in what follows that the general theory of tense will need to be able to capture the notion of future tense. Many languages, of course, lack this category, but this is in principle no different from most other categories in the general theory, e.g. many languages lack number as a grammatical category, but the general theory requires this category in order to handle those languages that do have a category of number. In European languages, in particular, the future tense seems to be weak or non-existent as a grammatical category (though substantiation of this point would require demonstration that future time reference can be deduced from other features of the meaning of the forms used to express future time reference). It is not impossible, however, that more detailed work on the tense systems of languages less well studied to date, such as indigenous languages of Africa and New Guinea, might lead us to change this assessment in favour of the more widespread occurrence of the future tense as a separate grammatical category.

2.4 Binary tense systems

In the previous sections of this chapter, we have established the validity of the notions present, past and future tense in general linguistic theory. Although we have illustrated each of these with actual linguistic examples, mainly though not exclusively from English, we have so far said little about tense systems internal to specific languages. While the general

---

[16] See further section 5.4 and Comrie (1982).

theory allows us a three-way distinction within absolute tense, many languages in fact have a basic two-way split, with either an opposition between past and non-past or between future and non-future.

Past versus non-past is, as mentioned in section 2.3, the basic tense split in many European languages, with sub-divisions within non-past (especially future as opposed to present) being at best secondary: thus the so-called present tense in such languages is frequently used for future time reference, and in such languages as Finnish is the basic means of expressing future time reference; conversely, the so-called future tense has modal uses which do not require future time reference, as with German *er wird schon da sein* 'he will already be there'. Within languages that make a basic past versus non-past distinction, it is worth distinguishing two sub-types, or at least two types which define end points on a continuum. The one would include languages where the present can always be used with future time reference, the only constraint on this use being avoidance of interpretations with present time reference. From Grice's maxim of relation (relevance), one would expect a non-past tense, other things being equal, to be given the interpretation of present time reference, since this is the interpretation most relevant to the situation at hand. German and Finnish would fall into this category. At the opposite extreme would be languages where, although the present can be used with future time reference, there are severe constraints on this use of that form, constraints that are not explainable purely as strategies to avoid conversational implicatures. English would be an example of this category, since the present can be used with future time reference only under highly specific circumstances; in main clauses, as observed in section 2.3, only where the situation in question is presented as being scheduled.

Turning to the possibility of a future versus non-future binary split, it is important to be able to distinguish this as a tense split from a split which is occasioned primarily by mood, but gives the impression of a tense split because of the implicature links between certain modal and time reference oppositions. Thus, in Dyirbal, for instance, although it would at first appear that there is a split between future and non-future, investigation suggests rather that there is a distinction between realis and irrealis, with future and (most) present time reference happening to be on opposite sides of the dividing line. Nonetheless, Hua, one of the few New Guinea languages for which we have a really detailed description, does seem to present an incontrovertible example of a language with a clear and basic tense opposition between future and non-future; while there are various sub-divisions within the future, primarily of a modal nature, all have future time reference, and thus contrast with the non-future, which never has future time reference.[17]

Given the existence of binary past/non-past and future/non-future splits, the question might arise as to whether it is possible to have a present/non-present split, with a single non-present category covering time reference in the past and future to the exclusion of the present. Although there are some languages where there are similarities between the past and the future that are not shared by the present, I am not aware of any example of a language which has a clear-cut system opposing non-present as a single category to present. Thus in Buin, the same morphological form is used for both future and recent past (today past) time reference; in the former, however, the particle *toi* must be present, so there is a distinction between *ŋkoti* 'I saw (earlier on today)' and *toi ŋkoti* 'I will see'.[18] This would suggest a possible universal of tense systems: in a tense system, the time reference of each tense is a continuity. If this universal can be maintained in general, then it would exclude the possibility of discontinuous tenses; for a possible exception, see the discussion of Burera in chapter 4.

2.5 Tenseless languages

Our stated aim in this book is to provide a theory of tense which is sufficiently flexible to accommodate tense distinctions that recur across the languages of the world, while being sufficiently constrained to exclude logically possible distinctions that are not in fact possible in human language. Thus the universals established relate to the possibilities cross-linguistically, and do not imply that any given language has to make any of the distinctions set up within the overall framework (although there must be languages somewhere that make the distinction). In section 2.4, we saw that some languages do not make the present/future distinction, while other languages do not make the past/non-past distinction. The question now arises whether there are any languages which make neither of these distinctions, i.e. which lack absolute tense altogether. One could then generalise the question to relative tense, and ask whether there are any languages that lack tense altogether.

Indeed there are such languages. We will illustrate this point with examples from one such language, Burmese.[19] In this language, there are

---

[17] Haiman (1980: 140–144).

[18] I am grateful to Donald C. Laycock for information on Buin.

[19] Okell (1969: 173, 354–357, 424–428); although the first of these page references uses the terms future and non-future, the more detailed discussion of the second and third page references clarifies the essentially modal, rather than temporal, distinction. I have benefited from discussion of the Burmese data with Mary Cameron.

two sets of sentence-final particles that will be relevant to our discussion (the choice of an individual particle within one of these two sets is determined by considerations not germane to the present issue): realis *te/thǎ/ta/hta* and irrealis *me/mǎ/hma*. The realis particle can only be used on sentences that have present or past time reference (with no grammatical distinction between past and present time reference), and so might seem to be an indicator of non-future tense, as in the following examples: *sǎneinei-taiñ mye? hpya?-te* 'Saturday-every grass cut-*te*', i.e. '(he) cuts the grass every Saturday'; *da-caúñmoú mǎ-la-ta* 'that-because:of not-come-*ta*' 'because of that (they) didn't come'. For future time reference, the irrealis series of particles must be used, as in: *mǎne?hpañ sá-me* 'tomorrow begin-*me*', i.e. '(we) will begin tomorrow'. However, more detailed examination of the functions of the *me* series shows that time reference is not its prime function. It can be used with present or past time reference provided the reference is not restricted to our actual world, i.e. provided there is modal value to the particle: *hmañ-leíñ-me* 'be:true-undoubtedly-*me*', i.e. 'that may well be true'; *mǎcìthì sà-hpù-me htiñ-te* 'tamarind:fruit eat-ever-*me* think-*te*', i.e. '(I) think (he) must have eaten tamarinds before'. Note in particular the use of both particles in this sentence, realis *te* to indicate what I actually think, and irrealis *me* to indicate a supposition as to what he may have done – even though the time reference of the irrealis *me* is in fact prior to that of the realis *te*, indicating clearly that time reference is not basic to the opposition between these particles.

What Burmese shows us, then, is a language where time reference per se is not grammaticalised, i.e. there is no tense. It is, of course, possible for time reference to be expressed in other ways (for instance lexically, by the use of adverbials like *mǎne?hpañ* 'tomorrow'), and for deductions about time reference to be made from other aspects of the sentence, perhaps in conjunction with knowledge of the world, as when sentences with the irrealis particle are frequently interpreted to have future time reference. But all of this is without reference to any grammatical category that has future time reference as part of its meaning.

What has been said about Burmese could be extended equally to Dyirbal, where it seems that the usual time reference difference between the verb form in *-n(yu)* and the verb form in *-ny* is derivative of a more basic modal distinction between realis and irrealis respectively. It should be noted that, although we have used the same terms realis and irrealis in speaking both of Burmese and Dyirbal, the precise dividing line between them is different in the two languages. In Dyirbal, present habitual is expressed using the irrealis, whereas in Burmese it is treated as realis. What is common, however, to the two systems is that a basically modal opposition has implications for time reference without this time reference being grammaticalised in the language; differences between the modal systems of the two languages is a problem for a theory of mood, rather than for a discussion of tense.

So far, we have been speaking in this section of languages that lack tense distinctions. A further question to arise is the possibility of particular constructions that are tenseless in languages that basically do have tense oppositions. In many languages with tense distinctions, certain non-finite forms, in particular, lack tense oppositions. (Perhaps even more frequently, one finds languages where finite verb forms characteristically have absolute time reference, while non-finite verb forms have relative time reference; the theory propounded in this book treats both absolute and relative tense as sub-cases of tense – see chapter 3 – and we are therefore interested here strictly in constructions which show no tense opposition, not even relative tense distinctions.) In English, for instance, derived nominals show no tense distinction, so that *the enemy's destruction of the city* can be expanded as relating to either *the enemy destroys the city* or *the enemy destroyed the city* or *the enemy will destroy the city*. In many instances, the precise time reference of a tenseless construction will be deducible from the context. Thus, in English the infinitive after the verb *promise* shows no tense opposition, e.g. *John promised to give me ten pounds*. However, it is possible to deduce that the time reference of *to give me ten pounds* is to a time subsequent to the time of John's promise, i.e. relative future tense. This deduction has nothing, however, to do with the grammatical system of English, in particular with the grammatical expression of time reference. Rather it follows from our knowledge of promises, namely that they refer to a future situation, i.e. one can only make promises about things that are to happen in the future relative to the time of the promise.[20] This is not to deny that there is an important research endeavour in this area, to investigate how different facets of the structure of a sentence, the context, and knowledge of the world combine to enable one to make deductions about the time reference of situations. Much of this, however, is irrelevant to a theory of tense defined as grammaticalisation of time reference: tense is only one component in the overall expression of time reference, and while it has an important role to play in languages with tense oppositions, it is crucial not to

[20] Searle (1969: 57). Actually, relative time reference is possible in the infinitive after *promise*, as in *John promised to have finished before we returned*, where the perfect infinitive indicates relative past time reference; the past time reference is, however, relative to our returning, not to John's promising.

confuse the study of tense with the overall enterprise of investigating how information relating to time reference is conveyed; equally, it is important to realise that an accurate characterisation of tense oppositions is a crucial component of this larger enterprise.

It is also possible that the grammar of a language may take advantage of redundancies in time reference in order to provide simpler expressions. Thus, in the English example with *promise*, although the time reference of the infinitive after *promise* is relative future, this is redundant, since this is the only possible time reference for an infinitive after *promise*; no information is thus lost by having a tenseless construction after *promise*. While this interaction between time reference, redundancies, and tenseless constructions is, again, of great potential interest, it falls outside the scope of a theory of tense as such.

2.6 Combinations of absolute tenses

So far, each of the tenses we have examined has located a situation in a certain segment of the time line. Negative versions of these tenses simply indicate that the negative situation, i.e. the absence of the equivalent positive situation, holds a certain segment of the time line. Thus *John was not at the party* simply indicates that a certain situation, namely *John not be at the party* (which happens to be the negation of *John be at the party*), held at some time in the past. Crucially, it does not mean, nor imply, that the situation *John be at the party* held in the non-past (present or future); nor even does it exclude the possibility that at some other time in the past, John may have been at the party, any more than *John was at the party* implies that John was at the party from the beginning of time up to the present moment.

The question may therefore arise as to whether it is possible for a language to have a tense, in the strict sense of a single grammatical category, which indicates that a situation holds at one segment of the time line but does not hold at certain other segments of the time line; or a tense indicating specifically that a given situation holds at different segments of the time line. While such tenses seem to be extremely rare cross-linguistically, they are attested in a number of Bantu languages, the examples below being taken from Luganda.[21] Note that in all of these examples, it is still the case that the situation referred to occupies a continuous segment of the time line; the only difference is that explicit mention is made of the fact that this continuous segment is partially located at the present moment and partially at some other stretch of time continuous with present moment.

[21] Ashton et al. (1951: 229, 230).

Absolute tense

We may start our discussion with the 'still' tense, so called because its most natural translation into English is with the adverb *still*; in Luganda, this takes the tense prefix *kya-*, as in *mu-kya-tudde* 'you still sit', i.e. 'you are still seated', *ente tu-kya-gi-n-oonya* 'cow we-still-it-seek', i.e. 'we are still looking for the cow'. The temporal reference of this form thus combines past and present time reference: we were looking for the cow. Moreover, the reference must be to a single situation of looking for the cow, i.e. the 'still' tense of Luganda cannot be used to refer to distinct situations of searching for a cow in the past and searching for a cow in the present.

Further insight into the semantics of this tense can be gleaned from an examination of its negative form, e.g. *te-mu-kya-tudde* 'Neg-you-still-sit'. The precise meaning of this form is 'you are no longer seated', i.e. it was true in the past that you were seated, but at the present moment it is not true that you are seated. The negation thus attaches only to the present reference of the 'still' tense, but crucially does not negate the past time reference of this form; whence the name 'no longer' tense for this form in Luganda. What this clarifies is the distribution of presupposition and assertion in the 'still' tense.[22] Since negation affects only the present time reference part of the overall meaning of the 'still' tense, this indicates that the present time reference is the assertion of this tense, while the past time reference, which remains constant under negation, is a presupposition. Thus a more accurate semantic description of the 'still' tense would be: it is presupposed that a situation held in the past, and asserted that it holds at the present. Its negative would therefore automatically receive the interpretation: it is presupposed that a situation held in the past and asserted that it does not hold at the present.

Given the possibility of combining different time references in this way, a host of logically possible tenses are created, although to date very few have been attested in languages, and it may be that such forms are at the very edge of possibilities in natural language, although only further research will answer this question. Luganda has one further verb form that fits into this general pattern, namely the 'not yet' tense, as in *te-tu-nna-genda* 'Neg-we-not:yet-go', i.e. 'we have not yet gone'; this tense occurs only in the negative. The meaning of this tense is that a certain situation (in the example given, our going) did not hold in the past and does not hold in the present, i.e. that it still is the case that a certain situation does not hold. It may seem that there is an additional semantic component, namely that the situation of our going will hold in the future. However, further investigation shows that this is only an implicature, not part of the meaning of the

[22] For the term 'presupposition', see the discussion in Lyons (1977: 606).

verb form, as is equally the case with the English expression *not yet*. All that is indicated with regard to the future is the possibility of the situation holding in the future, and this possibility may be demonstrated as unrealisable by the rest of the context, as for instance with English *I haven't yet seen him, and don't ever expect to*. For Luganda, one can compare *tobala nnyumba zitannazimbwa* 'don't reckon in the houses which have not yet been built', where one of the reasons for not including those houses may well be that they will never be built.

3
Relative tense

3.1 **Pure relative tense**

In chapter 2 we illustrated absolute tense, whereby the reference point for the location of a situation in time is the present moment. We now turn to relative tense, where the reference point for location of a situation is some point in time given by the context, not necessarily the present moment. The phenomenon of relative tense will first be illustrated by examples from English: although English finite verb forms have absolute time reference in nearly all instances (for exceptions, see chapter 6), English non-finite verb forms characteristically have relative time reference. Subsequently, examples will be cited from other languages, in particular languages where relative time reference plays a more substantial role in the grammar overall, whether in non-finite constructions (e.g. Latin) or in finite constructions as well (e.g. Classical Arabic).

But before looking at relative tenses, in particular in contrast with absolute tenses, it will be useful to look at the conceptually identical distinction with time adverbials, since here it is somewhat easier to see precisely the factors involved. Some time adverbials serve specifically to locate a situation relative to the present moment, e.g. *today* (the day including the present moment), *yesterday* (the day preceding the day including the present moment), *tomorrow* (the day following the day including the present moment); in our terminology, these are all instances of absolute time reference.[1] In addition, there are (in general distinct) adverbials which locate a situation relative to some reference point given by the context, such as *on the same day, on the day before, on the next day*; in our terminology, these are all instances of relative time reference. In a sentence with an adverbial of relative time reference, such as *on the next day Jack looked out of his bedroom window*, one's natural reaction is to look for a

---

[1] The set of forms indicating, in our terminology, absolute time reference are called 'shifters' by Jakobson (1957); likewise, our term 'relative time reference' corresponds to his term 'connectors'.

reference point in terms of which this time adverbial can be interpreted – the next day after what? In a sentence with an adverbial of absolute time reference, this question does not arise: the time reference of *tomorrow Jack will look out of his bedroom window* is quite clear (though there may, of course, be problems in relating this time adverbial to other, non-deictic systems of time coordinates: if you don't know what day of the week, or what date it is today, then you won't be able to work out what day or date it is tomorrow).

As English illustrative material, we shall take uses of the participles corresponding to relative clauses, such as *the passengers awaiting flight 26 proceeded to departure gate 5*. One interpretation of this sentence in English is that the time reference of *awaiting* is simultaneous with the time reference of the main verb *proceeded*. Since the time reference of *proceeded* is past – as a finite verb, it receives absolute time reference – the time reference of *awaiting* is interpreted as simultaneous with that past moment in time. In many contexts, this sentence is thus informationally equivalent to the following sentence, with a finite subordinate clause: *the passengers who were awaiting flight 26 proceeded to departure gate 5*. It is important, however, to note that this equivalence is at best in interpretation: the meanings of the two sentences are subtly but crucially different. One difference is that the version with the participle establishes simultaneity between the time reference of the participle and the time reference of the reference point (which in the interpretation under discussion is taken to be the time reference of the main verb *proceeded* – but for other possible interpretations, see below), while the version with the finite verb merely locates the time reference of the awaiting as being in the (absolute) past, without equating it with any other point of time in the past. It is thus possible, though pragmatically less likely, that the past time points at which *were awaiting* and *proceeded* are located in this sentence are different time points in the past.

The second difference is that identification of the time reference of *awaiting* with that of *proceeded* is only one possible interpretation of the participial clause. Another interpretation is that the reference is to passengers who are now, at the present moment, awaiting flight 26, an interpretation that is not available for the supposed paraphrase with a finite verb in the past tense. In fact, the finite clause paraphrase for this second interpretation would be *the passengers who are awaiting flight 26 proceeded to departure gate 5*. One would need to build up a more specific context for this interpretation of the participial construction to make sense, for instance a context where it becomes relevant to discuss the previous itinerary of those passengers who are now waiting for flight 26, but once this extra context is provided, the interpretation becomes perfectly natural.

This second interpretation might suggest that the English present participle is ambiguous between relative time reference (as in the first interpretation) and absolute time reference (as in the second interpretation). There is evidence, however, that this analysis is incorrect. It is possible for the same sentence to be given an interpretation where the time reference of the participle is simultaneous neither with the assigned time reference of the main clause nor with the present moment, if some other time point is given by the context as reference point. The easiest way of establishing such a reference point is to insert an adverbial of temporal location into the participial construction, as in *the passengers awaiting flight 26 yesterday proceeded to gate 5 the day before*, where the adverbial *yesterday* provides a reference point for the interpretation of the temporal location of the participle *awaiting*. It is also possible that the reference point might be given by the wider context. Thus, suppose someone asked about the passengers who had been awaiting various flights yesterday, in order to find out what gate they had proceeded to on their flight of the previous day. In this context, the partial answer *the passengers awaiting flight 26 proceeded to gate 5* would receive as its only coherent interpretation *the passengers who were awaiting flight 26 yesterday proceeded to gate 5 the day before*.

This suggests that for relative tenses all that is required is the identification of a reference point, the range of potential reference points being in principle all those compatible with the given context. Thus, the present moment is, unless barred by context, always available as a reference point for relative tenses. This means that a relative tense is quite strictly one which is interpreted relative to a reference point provided by the context; since the context always provides the present moment (unless some other feature of the context excludes this interpretation), an interpretation is always possible for relative tenses whereby they are apparently interpreted absolutely, but this apparent absolute interpretation is illusory. The difference between absolute and relative tense is not that between the present moment versus some other point in time as reference point, but rather between a form whose meaning specifies the present moment as reference point and a form whose meaning does not specify that the present moment must be its reference point. Relative tenses thus have the present moment as one of their possible reference points, but this is a problem of interpretation rather than of meaning.

Given that the most salient interpretation, barring contextual indications to the contrary, for relative tense is simultaneity with the closest absolute tense form, the relativity of time reference of English participles can be shown by varying independently the time reference of the closest finite verb and the time reference of the participle. The present participle is always interpreted as simultaneous with the reference point, as in the following informationally-equivalent paraphrases: *the passengers awaiting flight 26 must proceed to gate 5* (i.e. *the passengers who are awaiting flight 26 . . .*); *the passengers awaiting flight 26 will proceed to gate 5, starting next week* (i.e. *the passengers who will be awaiting flight 26 . . .*).[2]

If the participle is changed to the past participle, e.g. active *having boarded* or passive *(having been) denied boarding*, then we get relative past time location, as in *the passengers denied boarding on flight 26 proceeded to gate 7*. One interpretation takes the reference point to be defined by the time location of *proceeded*, giving the informationally equivalent paraphrase *the passengers who had been denied boarding proceeded to gate 7*, where the pluperfect (see section 3.2) indicates that the denial of boarding preceded the proceeding to gate 7. Other interpretations, with other contextually given reference points, are also possible, for instance *the passengers who have (just recently) been denied boarding proceeded to gate 7 yesterday*, where the present moment is taken as reference point; or *the passengers who had been denied boarding up to the day before yesterday proceeded to gate 7 yesterday*, if the context provides information to make such an interpretation likely.

Changing the main verb in tense, but keeping the past participle, gives sentences like *pasengers denied boarding on flight 26 should proceed to gate 7*, with its most likely interpretation *passengers who have been denied boarding . . .*, and *passengers denied boarding on flight 26 will proceed to gate 7*, with as its most likely interpretation *passengers who will have been denied boarding . . .*,[3] but also other interpretations, such as *passengers who have up to now been denied boarding . . .*, rather than *passengers who have been denied boarding up to the time of proceeding to gate 7 . . .*.

English does not have straightforward non-finite forms with future time reference, although constructions like *about to* come close. (They differ from mere future time reference in that they refer to immediate future,

---

[2] Note that English allows the present tense in finite relative clauses simultaneous with a future main clause, i.e. *the passengers who are awaiting flight 26 will proceed to gate 5, starting next week*; for some discussion of such examples, which involve a further parameter independent of the present discussion, see chapter 6.

[3] In more normal English, this would read *passengers who have been denied boarding . . .*; for the perfect rather than the future perfect, cf. the discussion of the present rather than the future in footnote 2.

rather than any future, and in that they indicate a propensity to a future situation rather than strictly a future situation as such – see further chapter 4.) This gives examples like *passengers about to depart on flight 26 proceeded to gate 5*, with as one interpretation that the passengers were about to depart on flight 26 when they proceeded to gate 5, but also a possible interpretation that those who are now about to depart on flight 26 proceeded at some time in the past to gate 5, or even that those who at some other specified time were or will be about to depart on flight 26 proceeded at some time in the past to gate 5. Changing the tense of the main verb gives *passengers about to depart on flight 26 should proceed to gate 5* (most likely interpretation: *those now about to depart . . .*), and *passengers about to depart on flight 26 will, from next week, proceed to gate 5* (most likely interpretation: *from next week, those who will be about to depart . . .*).

In the following examples from other languages, we shall restrict ourselves to interpretations where the reference point is taken to be that established by the tense of the closest verb with absolute time reference, as this is usually the most salient interpretation and also the one intended by the particular examples given in our sources; our claim, however, would be that these sentences should have a range of interpretations similar to those given for English.

In Latin, use of participles as substitutes for finite subordinate clauses is much more frequent than in English, and the richness of the system is enhanced by the existence of a specifically future participle, although widespread use of this form in this way is moie characteristic of post-classical Latin.[4] While the Latin finite verb forms receive absolute time reference (past, present, or future time reference – for the pluperfect and future perfect, see section 3.2), the participles receive relative time reference, normally by reference to the time established by the main verb. Thus, the present participle has relative present time reference, as in *Serviō Tulliō rēgnante viguērunt* (Cicero) 'Servius Tullius reigning, they flourished', i.e. 'they flourished when Servius Tullius ruled'; *omnēs aliud agentēs, aliud simulantēs perfidī* (Cicero) 'all other-thing done, other-thing pretending treacherous', i.e. 'all who drive at one thing and pretend another are treacherous' – in this second example the main clause has present time reference, indicated by the zero copula, so the present participles most naturally receive the interpretation of simultaneity with this present reference point established by the main clause.

The past participle has relative past time reference: *Mānlius Gallum caesum torque spoliāvit* (Livy) 'Manlius Gaul having-been-killed neck-

---

[4] The Latin examples are from Gildersleeve & Lodge (1895: § 664–670).

chain-from stripped', i.e. 'Manlius stripped the Gaul who had been killed of his neckchain'; *sī latet ars, prōdest; affert dēprēnsa pudōrem* (Ovid) 'if hides art, does-good; brings having-been-detected shame', i.e. 'if art hides, it does good, if it has been detected, it brings shame'. The future participle has relative future time reference: *trāiectūrus Rhēnum commeātum nōn trānsmīsit* (Suetonius) 'about-to-cross Rhine provisions not sent-across', i.e. 'when he was about to cross the Rhine, he did not send over the provisions'; *quatiunt arma, ruptūrī imperium nī dūcantur* (Tacitus) 'clash arms, about-to-break order if-not they-are-led', i.e. 'they clash their arms, ready to break orders if they are not led forward'.

In Imbabura Quechua, main clause verbs receive absolute time reference, while most subordinate clause verbs receive relative time reference, as in the following examples:[5] *Marya Agatupi kawsajta* (present) *krirkani* (past) 'I believed that Mary lived in Agato'; *Marya Agatupi kawsashkata* (past) *krirkani* (past) 'I believed that Mary had lived in Agato'; *Marya Agatupi kawsanata* (future) *krirkani* (past) 'I believed that Mary would live in Agato'; *yani* (present) *Marya mishu shimita parlajta* (present) 'I believe that Mary speaks Spanish'; *Juzika ñuka kaya llamata randinata* (future) *kri-n* 'Joseph believes that I will buy a sheep tomorrow'.

In looking for examples of relative time reference, it is essential to ensure that the relative time reference interpretation is part of the meaning of the form in question, rather than an implicature derived from, in part, the context. One area which is particularly confusing in this respect is narrative, where one gains the impression of a sequence of events which are located temporally one almost immediately after the other, the chronological sequence mirrored in the linear order of clauses. Thus one might be tempted to think that this sequencing is part of the meaning of the verb forms used, thus introducing a meaning of 'immediate past' or 'immediate future' relative time reference (depending on whether one defined the time reference of the preceding verb in terms of the following verb, or vice versa). However, as was shown in section 1.8, this sequencing of events is a property of narrative itself, quite independent of the verb forms used to encode narrative, so that the mere fact that verb forms receive this interpretation in narrative is not sufficient evidence for assigning this meaning to those verb forms. Indeed, crucially one would need to look for examples outside of narrative, where the context does not force the

---

[5] Cole (1982: 34–37, 142–143). Note that time interpretation in relative clauses is absolute, not relative. Note also that the suffixes for absolute and relative tense are distinct in Imbabura Quechua.

Relative tense

immediate succession interpretation, to demonstrate that this is actually part of the meaning of the forms in question. For further discussion of immediate past and immediate future, reference should be made to chapter 4.

This property of narrative may also be used to explain the immediate past time reference interpretation often assigned to the English present participle in narrative contexts, although we have claimed that the meaning of the English present participle is relative present time reference. An example would be *crossing the street, I entered the supermarket*, where the only possible interpretation, given our knowledge of possibilities in the world and relative locations of buildings and streets, is that I first crossed the street and then entered the supermarket, without any overlap between the two situations.[6] The sequencing which is part of the definition of narrative provides a moving reference point of time, and thus the present participle in narrative sequence is interpreted as simultaneous with the current reference point, i.e. immediately prior to the reference point defined by the next verb/ event in the narrative sequence. Languages which have explicit means for indicating relative time reference may differ in the extent to which such means are used where the context otherwise makes clear the chronological relation: thus English allows *after crossing* [or: *having crossed*] *the street, I turned right,* whereas French requires *après avoir traversé la rue, j'ai tourné à droite.*

In the languages investigated so far, relative time reference has been restricted to subordinate verb forms (finite or non-finite), while main clause (and many subordinate clause) verb forms have received absolute time reference. It should be noted, however, that these correlations are by no means absolute across the languages of the world. Taking first the correlation between subordinate verbs and relative time reference, we have already noted that subordinate finite verb forms in English nearly always receive absolute time reference. In some languages even some non-finite verb forms receive absolute time reference. Russian, for instance, has imperfective past participles in -*vš*-. While other participles in Russian receive relative time reference, much as in English, this participle receives absolute time reference, as in *ljudi, čitavšie žurnaly, ničego ne zametili* 'the people who were reading [literally: having read] magazines noticed nothing'; since the present participle has relative present time reference, this sentence is

---

[6] Note that the version *having crossed the street, I entered the supermarket* is also possible, though rather pedantic for a narrative context where sequencing is expected, especially given that the present participle could hardly be misinterpreted as indicating simultaneity in this example.

62

informationally equivalent to the same sentence with substitution of the present participle for the past participle: *ljudi, čitajuščie žurnaly, ničego ne zametili* 'the people reading magazines noticed nothing'.

Turning now to the correlation between main clause verbs and absolute time reference, there are some languages where even main clause verbs receive relative time reference, for instance Classical Arabic.[7] Arabic has morphologically an opposition between two verb tense-aspects, conventionally called imperfect and perfect. In addition to aspectual values, the imperfect has the time reference meaning component of relative non-past, while the perfect has the time reference meaning component of relative past. In neutral contexts, i.e. where no reference point is given explicitly by the context, the reference point is taken to be the present moment, thus giving the impression of absolute non-past meaning for the imperfect but past meaning for the perfect. However, if the context indicates some other point as reference point, then the basic relative time reference meaning of the verb forms surfaces, as in *wa ttabaʕū* (perfect) *mā tatlū* (imperfect) *'l-šayāṭīnu ʕalā mulki sulaymāna* 'and they followed what the demons used to recite in Solomon's reign', where the past time reference interpretation of the imperfect verb *tatlū* is established by the time adverbial 'in Solomon's reign'; *ʔajīʔu-ka* (imperfect) *ʔiðā 'ḥmarra* (perfect) *'l-busru* 'I will come to you when the unripe date ripens', where the subordinate verb is perfect because its time reference is past relative to that of the main clause (i.e. first the date will ripen, then I will come to you).

Since, as we have seen in various examples, relative tenses are often interpreted with the present moment as the reference point, especially where there is no other reasonable reference point given by the context, this suggests a strategy for the analysis of single verb forms that receive both apparent relative and apparent absolute time reference interpretations: given that the apparent absolute time reference interpretation can often be subsumed as a special case of relative time reference, the strategy would be to assume that the basic meaning of the form in question, indeed perhaps the only meaning of the form, is relative time reference, with the apparent

---

[7] Wright (1898: 1–24). It should be noted that the reference here is strictly to Classical Arabic, and not to Modern Standard Arabic, in which, as generally in the vernaculars, the so-called imperfect has basically non-past time reference, and requires the auxiliary verb *kaana* 'be' in the so-called perfect to be used for past imperfective time reference, even in the presence of a time adverbial explicitly indicating past time. In Modern Standard Arabic and the vernaculars finite verb forms receive relative time interpretations only in very restricted circumstances, usually only when accompanying a main verb with absolute time interpretation; see, for instance, the discussion of Maltese in section 3.2. For information on Modern Standard Arabic tense and aspect, I am grateful to Maurice Salib.

absolute time reference just a contextually dependent interpretation thereof. Of course, it would be necessary to check further the analysis that results from the application of this strategy, for instance by seeing whether the allegedly relative tense is compatible with time adverbials that would be incompatible with it on its absolute time reference interpretation: this is the argument we used above for saying that Classical Arabic has relative tense (the imperfect can collocate with adverbials indicating a specific period in the past), while in Modern Standard Arabic and vernacular Arabic reflexes of this form have absolute time reference.

The observation of the previous paragraph might suggest a re-analysis of some problems that we discussed in section 1.8, namely the possibility of the German perfect and the Portuguese preterite having future time reference, as in German *morgen bin ich schon abgefahren* 'tomorrow I will already have left' (literally: 'tomorrow I am already left'), Portuguese *quando você chegar, eu ja saí* 'when you arrive, I will already have left' (literally: '. . . I already left'). One might argue that these forms actually have relative past time reference, with an absolute time interpretation being assigned only where the context does not explicitly specify some other reference point, as in *ich bin abgefahren, saí* 'I've left'. More detailed investigation shows, however, that this suggested re-analysis is incorrect. In particular, it is only possible for the apparent relative time reference to occur relative to a reference point in the future, but not to a reference point in the past, where these verb forms simply receive their normal past tense interpretations. Thus *gestern bin ich abgefahren, saí ontem* can only receive the interpretation 'I left yesterday', where *yesterday* defines the point of my departure, and not 'yesterday I had left', where *yesterday* defines the past reference point prior to which I had departed – in other words, it is not possible to establish a past reference point contextually and then use these verb forms to locate a situation prior to this past reference point. Thus our earlier analysis still stands, whereby the non-distinction of present and future in German and Portuguese carries over to a non-distinction between future perfect and past, giving forms with basically past tense meaning (absolute tense), but a secondary meaning of location in time prior to a reference point in the future, provided the context defines such a reference point. Crucially, it is not the case that these verb forms can be used to indicate location in time prior to an arbitrary reference point.

3.2 **Absolute-relative tense**

So far, we have examined tenses with absolute time reference, where a situation is located at, before, or after the present moment; and relative tenses, where a situation is located at, before, or after a reference point given by the context. The next question to arise is whether it is possible for a single verb form to combine these two kinds of time reference, in other words, to have as part of its meaning that a reference point is situated at, before, or after the present moment and in addition that a situation is located at, before, or after that reference point. One of the most interesting empirical results of detailed work on tense is that such tenses do exist, indeed are very widespread across the languages of the world. They may be termed absolute-relative tenses, since their meaning combines absolute time location of a reference point with relative time location of a situation – although it should be noted that this is not a traditional term. (Traditional terminology, to the extent that it talks about absolute versus relative time reference, tends to group strict relative and absolute relative tenses together as 'relative'.) Within the framework espoused here, the possible absolute-relative tenses are determined by a reference point being before or after the present moment, and by the situation being located before or after that reference point. A reference point coinciding with the present moment simply gives absolute time reference, not absolute-relative time reference; a situation being located at a reference point in the past or future is likewise not distinguishable in terms of time location from absolute time reference.[8]

The notion of absolute-relative tense may be illustrated by examining the pluperfect in English. The meaning of the pluperfect is that there is a reference point in the past, and that the situation in question is located prior to that reference point, i.e. the pluperfect can be thought of as 'past in the past'. Note that all the tense means as far as reference point is concerned is that there is a reference point in the past; establishment of this reference point has to be done by examining the context. Often, the reference point is given by a time adverbial, as in *John had arrived by six o'clock yesterday evening*, where the time adverbial *by six o'clock yesterday evening* establishes a reference point in the past (6.00 pm yesterday), and John's arrival is located prior to that time point. The reference point may be given by a main clause to which the clause containing the pluperfect is subordinate, as in *when John had left, Mary emerged from the cupboard*, where the past tense of the main clause defines a reference point in the past (namely, the time of Mary's emerging from the cupboard), and John's leaving is located prior to this. The clauses can also be in the inverse relation, as in

---

[8] For a conflicting viewpoint, reference should be made to Reichenbach (1947). Some of the reasons for my rejection of Reichenbach's viewpoint are discussed below (see also chapter 6), and a more comprehensive discussion is given in Comrie (1981).

John had already left when Mary emerged from the cupboard, where once again it is Mary's emerging from the cupboard that defines a past reference point relative to which John's leaving is located. Or the reference may be given more generally by the context, as in a sequence of independent clauses like *the clock struck ten; John had already left*, where the first clause defines the reference point in the past, and the pluperfect of the second clause locates John's leaving prior to that reference point.

Although time adverbials often establish a reference point for the pluperfect, it should be emphasised that time adverbials co-occurring with the pluperfect do not necessarily establish a reference point, but may also encode the time at which the situation is located.[9] Thus the time adverbial in a sentence like *John had already left at ten o'clock* can receive two possible interpretations: the first, that ten o'clock is the reference point prior to which John had left; the second, that ten o'clock is the time at which John left (in which case the reference point must be sought elsewhere in the context). The broader context will usually make clear which interpretation is intended. In the following example, for instance, where the preceding clause establishes a reference point of midnight, the adverbial *at ten o'clock* is forced to take on the interpretation of the time of John's departure: *the clock struck twelve; John had already departed at ten o'clock*. In the next example, however, for the text to make sense *at ten o'clock* must be interpreted as the reference point prior to which John had left: *Mary came to visit John at ten o'clock; but John had already left at ten o'clock*.

It is important to note that, just as with pure relative tense, it is the context that gives the reference point for an absolute-relative tense. All that the meaning of the absolute-relative tense gives is the location of the reference point relative to the present moment, while any finer specification, down to the identification of the precise time point in question, is left to the context. Thus, while one can set up reasonable categories of where to look for the reference point of the pluperfect, these are at best heuristics, and not formal properties of the pluperfect or its meaning. Even a slight change in context can change the identification of the reference point. Thus, the clause sequence *John arrived; Mary had already left* will most naturally be given an interpretation where John's arrival is the past reference point relative to which Mary's departure is prior. Adding another clause, however, shifts this interpretation: *John arrived; Mary had already left before I arrived*. In this example, my arrival in the past is more likely to be taken as the reference point prior to which Mary left. Since the time relation between John's arrival and my arrival is left unspecified, it is not

---

[9] Pace Reichenbach (1947: 294).

possible to relate Mary's departure to John's arrival chronologically. If one assumes that this is a narrative, then the past tenses are most likely to be interpreted as sequential, i.e. John arrived before I arrived. But since Mary's departure preceded my arrival, this still leaves open whether Mary left before John's arrival, or between John's arrival and my arrival, and addition of other context may favour either one of these interpretations. The meaning of the pluperfect is thus restricted to location in time before a reference point that is located before the present moment, and everything beyond this is interpretation, and heavily context-dependent.

Since the pluperfect indicates a time point before some other time point in the past, it follows that the situation referred to by the pluperfect is itself located in the past. Thus time points that can be referred to by the pluperfect can in principle also be referred to by the past; this is not, incidentally, true, mutatis mutandis, of all absolute-relative tenses, and we shall see below that there is no absolute tense that can replace all instances of the future perfect, for instance. One might then ask, given that any past time point can be referred to by the past, why a pluperfect, with its relatively complex meaning, should exist in addition in so many languages. The answer is that, in locating situations in time, it is necessary not only to relate situations relative to the present moment, but also to relate them chronologically to one another. A simple sequence of past tenses fails to do this, e.g. *John arrived; Mary left*, which leaves open whether John's arrival preceded or followed Mary's departure. Given the tendency for linear order of clauses to follow chronological order of events, the example just given is most likely to be interpreted as meaning that John's arrival took place first, then Mary's departure. If for some reason it is desired to present events in other than chronological order, the pluperfect is an ideal mechanism for indicating this, as when the previous example is changed to *John arrived; Mary had left*.

Although many languages are like English in having a distinct pluperfect, there are also languages which lack any form with this meaning. Russian, for instance, has only absolute tenses (with relative tenses for a very restricted set of non-finite participles): present, past, and future. In Russian, then, it is necessary to use other devices to indicate that a given past event is not in its expected chronological sequence, i.e. the chronological sequence that would be expected from its linear position in the text. In Russian, the sequence of past tenses *Kolja priexal; Maša uexala* 'Kolya arrived; Masha left' will, as with past tenses in English, normally be assigned the interpretation that first Kolya arrived, then Masha left. If it is desired to present the events in this order linguistically, but with the reverse chronological interpretation, it is necessary in Russian to step outside the grammatical system of indicating time reference, for instance by using the adverb *uže* 'already', to give *Kolja priexal*; *Maša uže uexala*, literally 'Kolya arrived; Masha already left', a tense collocation that is rather jarring in English, where, even with inclusion of *already* the pluperfect would be preferred: *Kolya arrived; Masha had already left.*

In defining the meaning of the pluperfect we have emphasised the importance of the reference point in the past for felicitous use of the pluperfect. This is particularly important in distinguishing the pluperfect from other verb forms that have often identical interpretations, but on the basis of very different semantics, in particular remote past tenses (see further chapter 4). A number of languages have verb forms that are structurally reminiscent of the English pluperfect, by having the past tense of an auxiliary verb and a past participle, but whose interpretation is not, or at least is not necessarily that of locating a situation prior to a reference point in the past, but rather simply indicating that the time location of the situation is in the remote, rather than the close, past. Such languages include Hindi-Urdu and Armenian (Modern Eastern),[10] also some of the pidginized varieties of English spoken in West Africa.[11] As discussed in section 1.7, the fact that the pluperfect locates a situation prior to a reference point already in the past can often create an impression of a more remote past than would the simple past tense; however this is an implicature that can easily be cancelled, as in *this particle had been created 10^{-6} seconds before this other particle was created 10^{-9} seconds ago.* In fact pluperfect can be distinguished from remote past in two ways. First, the temporal location of the pluperfect is not necessarily remote; all that is required is a reference point intervening between the past location of the situation referred to by the pluperfect and the present moment, and the intervals involved can be infinitesimally small. Secondly, the pluperfect does require such an intervening reference point, while the remote past does not: it simply indicates that a situation held at a considerable temporal distance from the present moment, without any need to specify any of what filled the interval between the situation and the present moment.

Thus despite similarities between pluperfect and remote past in many situations, there are also situations where they are crucially distinct: in English, use of a pluperfect to indicate temporal remoteness when there is no intervening reference point available from the context will simply

[10] For Hindi, see Kellogg (1893: § 790); for Armenian, Fairbanks & Stevick (1958: 243–244).
[11] My information on West African Pidgin English is from Larry Hyman (personal communication).

disorient the English speaker. In English, one cannot just point at the Great Wall of China and say *they had built a magnificent wall*, the length of the elapsed interval between the building of the Wall and the present moment notwithstanding. In Hindu-Urdu and Armenian, the form that most closely corresponds formally to the English pluperfect seems to have two meanings, related but distinguishable: on the one hand, it can indicate a situation located prior to a past reference point, and when used in this way it corresponds to the English pluperfect. It can also be used, however, for a remote past event even when there is no intervening reference point, and this clearly differs from the English use of the pluperfect; overuse of the pluperfect, precisely to indicate remoteness without an intervening reference point, is one of the salient characteristics of many varieties of Indian English, under the influence of the broader range of uses of the formally similar form in Hindi and some other languages of the sub-continent.

The future perfect has a meaning similar to that of the pluperfect, except that here the reference point is in the future rather than in the past. Thus *I will have left* indicates that there is a reference point in the future, and that my departure is located temporally prior to that reference point. Just as with the pluperfect, the reference point is to be deduced from the context: the meaning of the form says only that there must be such a reference point, and gives no indication of where the reference point should be sought. The reference point may be given by a time adverbial, as in *I will have finished this manuscript by the end of next month*, where *by the end of next month* establishes the reference point prior to which my finishing the manuscript is located. But equally, the reference point may be given more diffusely by the more general context as in the following sequence of clauses: *so you're not arriving here until Tuesday; unfortunately, I will have left* – although it is always, of course, possible to add further specification of the reference point in the same clause as the future perfect, e.g. . . . *I will have left by then.*

Just as with the pluperfect, a time adverbial indicating a specific point or period of time co-occurring with the future perfect may indicate the reference point, but may equally indicate the time of the situation, so that *I will have left at six o'clock* receives two possible interpretations: one where six o'clock is the time of my departure (as in *if you don't get here till seven o'clock, you won't see me, because I will have left at six o'clock*), the other where six o'clock is the reference point in the future prior to which my departure is located (as in *if you don't get here till six o'clock, you won't see me, because I will already have left at six o'clock*).

Just as languages lacking a pluperfect must sometimes resort to extra-grammatical devices to clarify the time reference of situations that in English could be encoded with the pluperfect, so too such languages, e.g. Russian, must use similar devices where English can use the future perfect. Thus English *you will arrive at seven, but I will have left*, could be rendered into Russian as *ty prideš' v sem', no ja ujdu do ètogo*, literally 'you will arrive at seven, but I will leave before that'. However, as we will see in the next paragraph, this Russian version is subtly different from the English version, because the Russian sentence explicitly locates my departure in the future, whereas the English sentence at best does this by conversational implicature.

With the pluperfect, from its meaning of situation prior to a reference point in the past, it is possible to deduce that the time reference of the situation is also in the past relative to the present moment (although there is no need to include this as part of the meaning; parallelism with the future perfect would suggest indeed that this should not be included as part of the meaning). For the future perfect, no such assignment of absolute time reference interpretation is possible. All that the future perfect indicates is a situation prior to a reference point in the future, allowing the situation to be located after the present moment, at the present moment, or before the present moment, as is indicated in figures 4–6. The truth of this claim may not be self evident, and there is certainly some prima facie evidence against the claim.[12] The future perfect combines readily with a time adverbial of

Figure 4. Future perfect with future interpretation of situation

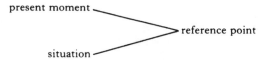

Figure 5. Future perfect with present interpretation of situation

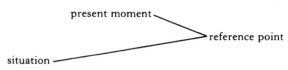

Figure 6. Future perfect with past interpretation of situation

[12] Hornstein (1977: 522, 526, 528–529) claims that the only representation for the future perfect is with the situation located between the present moment and the future reference

future time reference indicating the time of the situation (rather than of the reference point), as in *John will have finished tomorrow* (said in answer to the question whether or not John will be ready the day after tomorrow), while collocation with a time adverbial of present or past time reference is normally unacceptable, e.g. **John will have finished at this moment*, **John will have finished yesterday*. (We are speaking, of course, of the temporal, not the modal use of *will* – in the latter use, these sentences are fully acceptable.) In many instances, use of the future perfect in reference to a situation that has already taken place is clearly unacceptable: thus, if I know that John has already finished his work, then it would be unacceptable for me to say *John will have finished his work by tomorrow*; rather I should say *John has already finished his work*. We will argue, however, that these observations, though true in so far as they go, do not impinge on the meaning of the future perfect, but can all be accounted for in terms of implicatures following from the meaning of the future perfect, the context, and general conversational maxims of a Gricean kind.

Let us start with the example *John will have finished his manuscript by tomorrow*. Let us suppose moreover that I do not know whether or not John has already finished his manuscript (or at least do not wish to reveal this knowledge), but I know (and am prepared to divulge) that he will have finished it by tomorrow – say, because he made a promise to this effect several days ago, and is judged by me to be reliable. Then there are three sets of circumstances in which I can felicitously and truthfully utter this statement. One set of circumstances is where John finishes his manuscript between the moment of my uttering this sentence and the reference point 'tomorrow'. The second is where John is in fact finishing his manuscript at this very moment, but I am unaware (or wish to give the impression that I am unaware) of this fact. The third is where John has already finished his manuscript, but I am unaware (or wish to appear unaware) of the fact. Thus the time reference of John's finishing his manuscript is left open as to whether it is future, present, or past relative to the present moment, the only stipulation being that it must be prior to the reference point in the future, the sine qua non of the future perfect.

Since the speaker's knowledge was introduced into the discussion, one may legitimately ask precisely what role this factor plays, since in our definition of the future perfect we made no reference to the speaker's

point. However, it is unclear to me whether Hornstein's notation makes claims about the range of time location interpretations of the future perfect (in which case it is clearly incorrect), or just about collocation with time adverbials. In any event, I will suggest below that even the adverbial collocation facts are less clear.

knowledge. This factor, as part of the context, comes into play, however, when we consider not only the meaning of the future perfect but also its implicatures. If I say *John will have finished his manuscript by tomorrow*, then clearly my interlocutor is interested in (or is believed by me to be interested in) whether or not John's manuscript will be ready tomorrow. Now, if I know that he has already finished his manuscript, then clearly the most relevant information that I can give my interlocutor is that John has already completed it – given the relative uncertainty of the future, it is better to be able to give a report on an already accomplished fact than to rely on a prediction, however firm. In other words, by Grice's maxim of quantity (more particularly: 'make your contribution as informative as is required'),[13] if the speaker knows that John has already finished his manuscript, he should give this information. If he gives less information, as he does in using the future perfect, then his interlocutor, assuming that the conversation is between cooperating partners, will naturally infer that the speaker does not have the more specific knowledge, i.e. will draw the implicature that John's manuscript is not yet finished. The claim that absolute future time reference is an implicature, rather than part of the meaning of the future perfect, means that the person who says *John will have finished his manuscript by tomorrow* while knowing full well that John has already finished his manuscript is not, strictly, lying (saying something that is false), but is being devious (allowing the hearer to draw an implicature which is, in fact, false).

As with implicatures in general, it is possible for the implicature of future time reference to be cancelled by the context. Thus, suppose someone asks me *will John have finished his manuscript by tomorrow?* Suppose moreover that I know that John has already finished his manuscript. Then I can reply *yes; in fact, he has already finished it.* The first part of my reply, *yes*, indicates that I maintain the truth of the proposition *John will have finished his manuscript by tomorrow.* Now, if part of the meaning of this proposition were that John's finishing his manuscript is located between the time of my speaking and tomorrow, the following part of my reply would be a contradiction. However, it is not, whence the absolute future time reference cannot be part of the meaning of the future perfect. In fact, the second part of the reply serves only to cancel the implicature, as the simple answer *yes* would engender the implicature that the manuscript is not yet finished. One can contrast the question cited above with the following question, uttered in the same circumstances: *will John finish his manuscript between now and tomorrow?* Here, the answer *yes* would be inappropriate, even if the second

[13] Grice (1975).

part of the reply is attached – indeed, the second part of the reply would directly contradict the *yes*, since the answer *yes* locates John's finishing his manuscript in the future, while the rest of the reply locates it in the past. Under these circumstances, the best answer to the question would be simply the statement *he's already finished it*, which does not accept the factually incorrect presupposition of the original question that John has not yet finished his manuscript.

With certain sentences, cancellation of the implicature may be extremely difficult, given the unlikelihood of the required context, but cancellation is always possible. Thus, since people are normally supposed to be aware of their own actions, the sentence *I will have finished my manuscript by tomorrow* would hardly ever be appropriate in circumstances where I have already completed my manuscript, and one would have to imagine bizarre circumstances to allow cancellation of the implicature – for instance, that the speaker habitually works in a drug-induced stupor, and thus literally may not know whether or not he has completed his manuscript. But the oddity of the context does not militate against the validity of our analysis, rather it confirms it: provided one can think up circumstances which cancel the implicature, the implicature is indeed cancelled.

It is, moreover, possible to contrive circumstances under which it is acceptable to collocate an adverbial with past time reference with the future perfect, in its temporal interpretation, although the context is necessarily quite complex, as it has to be reasonable to talk about a past situation in reference to a future deictic centre. Suppose that a group of people worked yesterday on building a new dam. Their work is not yet completed, so it is crucial that it should not rain before they complete the work, otherwise what they have built so far may be washed away. Unfortunately, rain has been forecast for tomorrow. Under these circumstances, one of the workers might remark *if it rains tomorrow, we'll have worked in vain yesterday.*[14] The use of the future perfect here is justified in that the situation is located in the past relative to a future reference point, since until tomorrow, when we ascertain whether or not it rains, it will be impossible to know whether or not our work has been in vain. The use of the past time adverbial *yesterday* is equally justified, since our work took place yesterday. What is interesting about this example is that the temporal location of our work is clearly in the past, namely yesterday, but the temporal location of our work in vain is less clear, since although the work took place yesterday, evaluation of the work as in vain cannot take place until tomorrow. But what is shown crucially by this example is that the future perfect is in principle collocatable

[14] For further discussion of such sentences, see Comrie (1982).

with a past time adverbial; the fact that most instances of this collocation are unacceptable says nothing about the meaning of the future perfect, but only about its implicature.

In other languages I have investigated that have a future perfect, this form behaves in exactly the same way as has just been described for English. In particular, the one form can have absolute future, present, or past time reference, although conversational implicatures restrict the circumstances in which the last two possibilities are realised. Moreover, there seems to be no language which has two or three distinct future perfects depending on whether or not the absolute time reference of the future perfect is future, present, or past. The account we have given of the future perfect, namely a meaning 'past relative to a future reference point', predicts just this set of facts, and this is therefore strong evidence in favour of this analysis, in particular over an analysis that would analyse the future perfect as ambiguous, or over one that would analyse it as having only representations where the situation is located between the present moment and the future reference point.[15] In section 6, a formalism will be proposed that captures this prediction.

In both the pluperfect and the future perfect, the situation is located in the past relative to a reference point. On grounds of symmetry, one might also expect to find verb forms where there is a situation located in the future relative to a reference point, with this reference point being either in the past or in the future. Although such grammatical forms seem to be rarer than the pluperfect and the future perfect cross-linguistically, no doubt reflecting the greater incidence of grammaticalised past time reference over grammaticalised future time reference, such forms do nonetheless exist.

A future in the future can be formed in Latin by using the future participle of the lexical verb in conjunction with the future tense of the auxiliary 'be', e.g. *datūrus erit*, literally 'about-to-give he-will-be'. This form refers to a situation of giving that is located in the future relative to some reference point that is itself in the future. The future in the future is thus the mirror image of the pluperfect; and just as the pluperfect can only receive an interpretation where the situation is located in the absolute past, so the future in the future can only receive an interpretation where the situation is located in the absolute future. The closest equivalents in English are periphrastic constructions like *he will be about to give*, although these are not merely future in the future because of the differences already noted

---

[15] Reichenbach (1947) analyses the future perfect as being three ways ambiguous (see further chapter 6), while Hornstein (1977) analyses it as having only the representation where the situation is located between the present moment and the future reference point.

between the *about to* construction and simple future time reference: *about to* indicates immediate futurity, so the form is rather an immediate future in the future.

More frequent cross-linguistically is a future in the past, although here there is the particularly acute problem of future forms having modal as well as temporal values. Thus the English form *would leave* is probably more often than not used with modal meaning, whence its usual name conditional, but it can also be used purely temporally.[16] Apparent examples would seem to be indirect speech, as in *he said he would leave*, where the time reference of *would leave* is to a situation located in the future relative to a contextually established reference point in the past, here established by the tense of the verb of the main clause. However, we will see in section 5.3 that English indirect speech does not provide a good frame within which to investigate crucial instances of absolute-relative time reference, so other examples must be sought. The clearest examples are those where there is a basic narrative sequence in the past, but some situation is then described which falls outside this narrative sequence by being further into the future. Thus the following example will serve: *John left for the front; he would never return.* Here, the first clause establishes a reference point in the past. The second clause then refers to a situation located in the future relative to that past reference point. Note that the absolute time reference of the verb in the second clause is not specified: in fact, the most reasonable interpretation here is that it holds across all time from John's departure for the front through the present moment to the end of time. Future in the past time reference, though with added semantic parameters, can be obtained also by using other periphrases with future time reference, such as *John was about to leave*, locating a situation of John's leaving in the immediate future relative to a past reference point.

Given that it is possible to locate a situation relative to a reference point that is in turn located relative to the present moment, one might wonder whether it is possible to build up more complex tenses with a chain of reference points. The answer is that conceptually it is possible to do so, but very few of these logical possibilities are grammaticalised in languages. In addition to the future in the past (so-called conditional), English also has

---

[16] But the traditional nomenclature varies considerably even for European languages. Thus French uses distinct terms conditionnel and futur au passé for modal and temporal uses, respectively, and prescribes quite dire penalties for those who fail to make the distinction. In Brazil, traditional grammar has decided on the apparently temporal term futuro do pretérito for both modal and temporal uses. Modal uses do seem to be more prevalent here than with the future, where the temporal term future has been accepted without question in most traditional grammars.

the conditional perfect which thus acquires a temporal interpretation of [[past in the future] in the past] (or future perfect in the past), as can be seen in the following example: *John left for the front; by the time he should return, the fields would have been burnt to stubble*. Here, the first clause establishes a reference point in the past, namely the time of John's departure. The second clause then establishes a second reference point in the future relative to the first reference point. The final clause, in whose time reference we are interested, locates a situation, namely the fields' turning to stubble, in the past relative to that second reference point.

Apart from the conditional perfect in a number of European languages, such more complex absolute-relative tenses are exceedingly rare. For some French speakers, it is apparently possible to go one further degree into the past by using so-called *temps surcomposés* 'super-compound forms', although native speaker judgements on these forms are not always unequivocal, and not all logical possibilities receive the expected interpretation. The following example is from Stendhal:[17] *quand il avait eu rassemblé les plus effrontés de chaque métier, il leur avait dit 'régnons ensemble'* 'when he had gathered the most advanced of each trade, he had said to them "let us rule together" '. Here, the verb of the first clause is one step further back into the past than the pluperfect, i.e. is a past in the past in the past, expressing a situation located in the past relative to the situation described in the main clause, which is itself in the pluperfect. In English, it is in principle possible to build up a series of reference points using periphrastic constructions, although it is hard to imagine circumstances in which one would need or want to oscillate between past and future reference points as in *John would have been about to have just been about to leave*.

One formal characteristic of absolute-relative tenses in many languages is their compositionality, i.e. one can identify morphological correlates of the various time relations involved. In English, for instance, if one takes the morphological indication of the past/non-past distinction to be the outermost layer, then this establishes the relation between present moment and (first) reference point, while successively inner layers establish relations between subsequent reference points leading eventually to the relation between the last reference point and the situation. Thus in the pluperfect *had gone* we have past relation between reference point and present moment, then past relation between situation and reference point. In the future perfect *will have gone* we have future (*will*) relation between reference point and present moment, then past relation (*have gone*)

---

[17] Imbs (1960: 131–135).

between situation and reference point. In the future in the past *would go*, we have past relation (past tense morpheme in *would*) establishing a reference point before the present moment, then future (*will*) relation established between the situation and the reference point. In the conditional perfect *would have gone* the morphological past tense of *would* establishes a reference point in the past relative to the present moment; the auxiliary *will* establishes a reference point in the future relative to the first reference point; and the past tense form *have gone* locates the situation in the past relative to the second reference point.

A similar pattern, though using rather different morphological means, obtains in Maltese, with the auxiliary verb 'be' establishing the reference point and the tense of the lexical verb establishing the location of the situation relative to the reference point. For the auxiliary, the relevant forms are past *kien* 'he was' and future *se jkun* 'he will be'; for the lexical verb 'kill', the relevant forms are past *qatel* 'he killed' and future *se joqtol* 'he will kill'. This gives pluperfect *kien qatel*, future perfect *se jkun qatel* (where *se jkun* gives the reference point in the future, and *qatel* location in the past relative to the reference point), conditional *kien se joqtol* (where the past reference point is given by *kien*, the future location by *se joqtol*).[18] The formes surcomposées in French are dependent on exploiting the possibilities of compositionality one step further than is done in English, where **he had had gone* is not possible. Even in French, however, the compositionality is not recursive, as it is not possible to say **il avait eu eu rassemblé*. This is one way in which fully grammaticalised analytic constructions differ from periphrastic constructions like English *to be about to, to have just*, which can be combined recursively to give formally impeccable combinations, even if it is difficult to compute their meanings or find a use for them.

Absolute-relative tenses are not, however, always compositional in this way. Thus, literary Portuguese has a simple pluperfect, for instance *falara* 'he had spoken', although the spoken language prefers the compound *tinha falado* (cf. *tinha* 'he had', *falado* 'spoken').

In particular, given these remarks on the compositionality of absolute-relative tenses in so many languages, and also the traditional terminology with the term perfect, the question arises how, if at all, the perfect should be integrated into the present discussion. Just as in many languages the

---

18 More generally in Maltese the past and future of auxiliary 'be' enable situations to be located farther into the past or the future, respectively. Thus *qed joqtol* means 'he is killing'; adding the past of 'be' gives *kien qed joqtol* 'he was killing', while adding the future gives *se jkun qed joqtol* 'he will be killing'. I am grateful to Donna Wagner for drawing the conditional form *kien se joqtol* to my attention.

pluperfect consists of the past tense of an auxiliary plus a past form of the lexical verb, so too the perfect often consists of the present tense of the auxiliary with a past form of the lexical verb, as in English: pluperfect *I had gone*, future perfect *I will have gone*, perfect *I have gone*. Despite the apparent formal similarity between perfect and absolute-relative tenses, and despite the fact that many linguists have treated all of these in a uniform way,[19] it will be argued here that the perfect is in fact radically different from the absolute-relative tenses, and should not be given a uniform treatment with them.

First, the perfect is distinct conceptually from the absolute-relative tenses. The latter serve to locate a situation in time relative to a reference point which is itself located in time relative to the present moment (with possible extensions for languages where chains of reference points are possible). In terms of location in time, however, the perfect is not distinct from the past. The past tense locates an event in time prior to the present moment. If one were to provide an analysis of the perfect analogous to that of the pluperfect and the future perfect, then one would say that the reference point for the perfect is simultaneous with the present moment, rather than being before the present moment (as for the pluperfect) or after the present moment (as for the future perfect). The situation in question would then be located in time prior to this reference point. In terms of location in time, however, this would give precisely the same result as the past, which also locates a situation as prior to the present moment. Thus, however perfect differs from past, it is not in terms of time location.[20]

Moreover, once we look in more detail at similarities and differences, across languages, between the perfect on the one hand and absolute-relative tenses on the other, it soon becomes clear that the differences are at least as pronounced as the formal parallelism.

This can be illustrated initially for English. One of the characteristics of the perfect in English is that it cannot collocate with a time adverbial referring to a specific time point or period in the past, e.g. **I have arrived yesterday*. Although this sentence clearly locates the time of my arrival as in the past by means of the perfect, yet still it is not possible to have a time adverbial referring specifically to the single point or period at which this event took place. It is important to note that the claim is not that no time adverbial is possible referring to the time of the situation in question. If the time adverbial is interpreted habitually, i.e. as referring to a class of time

---

[19] See, in particular, the literature stemming from Reichenbach (1947).

[20] For a more positive characterisation of the meaning of the perfect, see, for instance, Comrie (1976: ch. 3).

points/periods rather than just to a specific time point or period, then collocation is possible, as in *I have arrived at two o'clock* (i.e. there has been at least one instance in my life when I arrived at two o'clock), or *whenever I get here at two o'clock the boss has always left at one-thirty for lunch*; in the first of these examples, it is not possible to interpret the sentence with *at two o'clock* referring, for instance, specifically to two o'clock today. As was noted above, it is possible for the perfect to co-occur with a time adverbial having present time reference, or more accurately having time reference including the present moment, e.g. *the boss has now left*, or *the boss has gone out this afternoon*.

This constraint on the perfect in English does not, however, carry over to the absolute-relative tenses, in particular the pluperfect and the future perfect.[21] With the English pluperfect and future perfect, as already discussed on pages 65–9, it is possible for time adverbials to refer to the specific point or period of time at which the situation is located (in addition to being able to refer to the reference point). Thus *John had arrived on Tuesday* can be interpreted to mean either that Tuesday was the time of John's arrival (the rest of the context giving a reference point between Tuesday and the present moment), or that Tuesday is the reference point prior to which John's arrival is located. The first of these interpretations clearly distinguishes adverbial collocation possibilities of the pluperfect from those of the perfect in English. The future perfect behaves like the pluperfect, as in *John will have arrived on Tuesday*, where Tuesday is either the day of John's arrival, or the reference point prior to which John arrived.

Although the collocation restriction against perfect with time adverbials referring to specific times in the past seems to be rather idiosyncratic to English, so that this particular test does not necessarily generalise to other languages, it does still provide an instance of non-correspondence between the perfect and the absolute-relative tenses, especially given the extent to which English has been used as an example of a language providing parallelism between perfect and absolute-relative tenses. The instances of lack of parallelism between perfect and absolute-relative tenses discussed

---

[21] This observation undermines one of the main arguments given by Reichenbach (1947) for parallel treatment of perfect and absolute-relative tenses. Reichenbach claims that the perfect, pluperfect, and future perfect have, respectively, present, past, and future reference points, and that time adverbials must be construed as identifying the reference point, not the time of the situation. For the perfect this is correct (at least if one makes the corrective addition that only those adverbials referring to specific times, rather than classes of times, are at issue), but for the pluperfect and future perfect it is an unfortunate factual inaccuracy.

Relative tense

below using data from languages other than English are more readily generalisable.

One piece of evidence against the parallelism of perfect and absolute-relative tenses is that some languages have a distinct perfect while lacking a distinct pluperfect and future perfect, while others have a distinct pluperfect and future perfect but no perfect, while in yet others the formation of perfect on the one hand and absolute-relative tenses on the other does not show parallelism of compositionality. In Swahili, for instance, there is a perfect, e.g. *amesoma* 'he has read', where the prefix *me-* before the verb stem *som* indicates the perfect (*a-* is a class prefix, indicating a third person singular human subject, while *-a* is a mood suffix), but no pluperfect or future perfect. In Maltese, pluperfect (e.g. *kien qatel* 'he had killed') and future perfect (e.g. *se jkun qatel* 'he will have killed') exist, but there is no distinct perfect; the simple past tense *qatel* translates both English 'he killed' and 'he has killed'.[22] In Luganda, the perfect is a simple verb form, e.g. *tulabye* 'we have seen' (where *tu-*, *tw-* before a vowel, is the first person plural subject prefix), while the pluperfect and future perfect are compounds, e.g. *twali tulabye* 'we had seen'. Thus, although Luganda makes roughly the same distinction as English here, there is no formal parallelism between the perfect on the one hand and the absolute-relative tenses on the other.[23]

Another piece of evidence is that, even where one has apparent formal compositional parallelism between perfect and absolute-relative tenses, the function of the two series is sometimes radically different. A good example here is provided by Portuguese. In Portuguese, the pluperfect and future perfect, as in English, simply locate a situation prior to a reference point in the past or future, respectively. Both are formed with the auxiliary *ter* 'have', in the past and future respectively, with the past participle of the lexical verb.[24] This gives examples like *ele já tinha saído quando eu cheguei*

[22] Some Maltese speakers apparently have a form *jkun qatel*, with an interpretation something like 'he is habitually in the state of having killed', using the present habitual of the verb 'be' (except for the habitual, Maltese has a zero copula in the present tense) (Schabert 1976: 131–132). Since some speakers do not have this form, their variety of Maltese still serves as an instance of a language having pluperfect and future perfect but lacking a perfect. Even for speakers who do have *jkun qatel* as a perfect, its meaning does not exactly parallel that of the pluperfect and future perfect, since only the perfect is necessarily habitual.

[23] Ashton et al. (1951: 123, 293).

[24] Literary Portuguese also has a simple pluperfect, e.g. *falara* 'he had spoken', in addition to the compound pluperfect. Literary Portuguese can also use either *ter* or *haver* as auxiliary in the pluperfect and future perfect, but only *ter* in the perfect. Thus, in literary Portuguese not even formal parallelism of compositionality holds. In the spoken language, however, one does have this formal parallelism, since only forms with the auxiliary *ter* exist, e.g. *ele*

80

'he had already left when I arrived'; *ele já vai ter saído quando eu chegar* 'he will already have left when I arrive'. Compositionally parallel to this, one can use the present tense of the auxiliary *ter* with the past participle of the lexical verb, to give *ele tem estudado*, literally 'he has studied'. However, the meaning of this last form is completely distinct from that of the absolute-relative tenses. It refers to a situation that is habitual for a period of time starting in the recent past and continuing up to (but not necessarily including) the present moment; thus, *ele tem estudado muito ultimamente* would translate into English as 'he has been studying a lot recently'. This complex time reference plus habituality is not part of the meaning of the pluperfect or of the future perfect. In Portuguese, if one simply wishes to refer to a situation in the past that has present relevance, without including the complex of habituality and continuation of the situation up to the present moment, then the only possibility is to use the simple past, the notion of present relevance being given either contextually or by linguistic means other than the verb form. Thus, both 'I studied Portuguese' and 'I have studied Portuguese' will translate into Portuguese as *eu estudei português*.[25]

One can also add a diachronic dimension to this discussion, by showing that distinct diachronic changes frequently affect the perfect on the one hand and the absolute-relative tenses on the other. Good illustrative material is provided here by the historical development of the original perfect in spoken French and in spoken German (especially the spoken language of southern Germany and Austria). Originally, these languages had an opposition similar to that of English, with a distinction between a simple past (French *je chantai*, German *ich sang* 'I sang') and a compound perfect (French *j'ai chanté*, German *ich habe gesungen* 'I have sung'). and pluperfect and future perfect forms parallel in composition to the perfect (French *j'avais chanté*, German *ich hatte gesungen* 'I had sung'; French

---

tinha falado 'he had spoken', *ele tem falado* 'he has been speaking', *ele vai ter falado* 'he will have spoken'. Note that for explicit future time reference the spoken language prefers the auxiliary *ir* 'go' (cf. *vai* 'he goes'), rather than the literary synthetic future (e.g. *terá* '(he) will have').

[25] In the subjunctive mood, the form *ele tenha falado*, with the present subjunctive of the auxiliary *ter*, is closer in meaning range to the English perfect, e.g. *sinto que ele tenha saído* 'I regret that he has left'. However, the tense system of the Portuguese subjunctive is in general radically different from that of the indicative, so that where the indicative has the three-way opposition preterite *ele falou* 'he spoke', imperfect *ele falava* 'he used to speak', and perfect *ele tem falado* 'he has been speaking', all with past time reference, the subjunctive has only a two-way opposition between so-called imperfect *ele falasse* and perfect *ele tenha falado*, the difference between these two being conditioned largely by sequence of tenses rather than by semantics.

81

j'aurai chanté or *je vais avoir chanté,* German *ich werde gesungen haben* 'I will have sung').[26] In the course of time, however, the original perfect usurped the functions originally covered by the simple past, so that *je chantai* and *ich sang* have fallen out of use, with *j'ai chanté* and *ich habe gesungen* covering both English 'I sang' and 'I have sung'. This radical change in the relation of simple past and perfect has had no repercussions on the pluperfect and future perfect, which continue with their same form and function. Thus, diachronically, the perfect and the absolute-relative tenses bifurcate.

Interestingly, this gives rise to a synchronic system closely paralleling the meaning we have assigned to past, pluperfect and future perfect, as will be illustrated using the German forms. The past *ich habe gesungen* consists of the present tense of the auxiliary (giving a present reference point) and the past participle (locating the situation prior to that present reference point); the pluperfect uses the past tense of the auxiliary, giving a past reference point, while the past participle locates the situation prior to this past reference point; the future perfect uses the future of the auxiliary (giving a reference point in the future), with the past participle locating the situation prior to that reference point. Thus there is no reason to suppose that compositionality would link the perfect with the absolute-relative tenses rather than linking the past with them. Latin, incidentally, has a system very similar to that of spoken French and German both in terms of compositionality and meaning, e.g. *cantāvī* 'I sang, I have sung', *cantāveram* 'I had sung', *cantāverō* 'I will have sung' (for the inflections of the last two, compare imperfect *eram* 'I was' and future *erō* 'I will be'); although the form *cantāvī* is called perfect in traditional Latin grammar, it covers the range of spoken French *j'ai chanté* rather than of English *I have sung*. Diachronically, the Latin so-called perfect represents the merger of earlier non-perfect past and perfect, in both form and function, whereas French *j'ai chanté* represents the merger of these two functions, but consistently in the form of the earlier perfect.

In sum, then, apparent arguments in favour of treating the perfect as parallel to the absolute-relative tenses evaporate on closer examination, and give way to a number of arguments in favour of not analysing these two sets of verb forms in parallel fashion.

---

[26] The French situation is slightly more complex because in the non-perfect system there is an opposition between imperfect *je chantais* 'I used to sing' and preterite *je chantai* 'I sang', but since the imperfect does not participate in or interact with the change discussed it may safely be left out of account.

4
Degrees of remoteness[1]

The tense oppositions discussed so far enable us to locate a situation temporally either at, before, or after a reference point, and in turn to locate that reference point at, before, or after the present moment. So far, however, we have not discussed possibilities of locating situations more accurately before or after a given reference point, although in principle the elapsed time between the reference point and the situation could be either very short or very long. Lexically, and by using lexically composite expressions, it is, of course, easy to express such distinctions, as in *John arrived five minutes ago*; *this star went nova five million years ago*. In principle, given the use of lexically composite expressions, one can locate the situation with infinitesimal accuracy. The question that now arises is: to what extent is it possible to carry out more accurate time location by means of grammatical categories?

A large number of languages have no grammatical means of carrying out more accurate location in time. In German, for instance, there is no grammatical opposition that will give distinctions in remoteness in the past or in the future. There is also, however, a large number of languages where such distinctions are possible by grammatical means. Indeed, one can find languages from all parts of the world which make such distinctions, including western European languages, although prolific systems distinguishing several different degrees of remoteness tend to be more restricted in occurrence. Examples will be cited below, however, from languages of sub-Saharan Africa (especially Bantu languages), from Aboriginal languages of Australia, and from native languages of the Americas, in addition to less prolific systems of oppositions from European languages.

In studying degrees of remoteness in tense systems, it is essential to ensure that the distinction under discussion has degree of remoteness as part of its meaning, rather than just as an implicature deriving from other

---

[1] In the preparation of this chapter, I have benefited greatly from consultation with Östen Dahl; see also in particular Dahl (1984).

features of its meaning. Thus, in section 1.7, we noted that there is often an implicature derivable from the perfect that this grammatical form has more recent time reference than other past tenses, although this is not part of the meaning of the perfect but rather derivable as an implicature from its meaning of present relevance of a past situation. Likewise, we observed that the pluperfect is often interpreted as referring to a situation more distant in the past than other past tenses, but again this is merely an implicature deriving from part of the meaning of the pluperfect, which requires a situation to be located prior to a reference point which is itself in the past, thus giving the impression of a more distant past. Many grammars of less well-studied languages, unfortunately, do not make clear whether the degrees of remoteness systems they posit for the language in question are really part of the meaning of the grammatical form, or just usual interpretations, in which case they might well be implicatures. In this chapter, we shall cite, as the main examples, languages which have been sufficiently deeply studied with regard to time reference so that we can be reasonably certain that the claims about degrees of remoteness in the tense system are accurate, although occasionally, for comparative purposes, less fully substantiated examples from the literature will be cited.

In this connection, it should be noted that it is also possible for a temporal distance interpretation to be one of a number of meanings of a grammatical form, i.e. for this interpretation to be a separate meaning that is not deducible from any of the other meanings of the given form, either individually or in combination. In such cases, we shall say that temporal remoteness is one of the meanings of the form in question, and concentrate for present purposes on that meaning. Once again, the relation between perfect and recent past turns out to be relevant. In many languages, there is a form, which we shall call perfect, which has as one of its meanings present relevance of a past situation, but which also has an additional meaning of recentness. It is important to note that this is not the same as saying that recentness is an implicature of the present relevance meaning. If the latter were the case, then we would expect languages with perfects having the meaning of current relevance to behave alike with regard to implicatures of recentness, since the implicature should, by definition, be derivable automatically from the combination of the meaning of the grammatical form and the context. However, this is not the case.

In English, for instance, the perfect can be combined with only a handful of time adverbials referring to a specific moment of time in the past, all of which denote the very recent past, as in *I have just seen John, I have recently made John's acquaintance*. In some Romance languages, however, such as Spanish (at least for some speakers) and Limouzi, an Occitanian dialect,[2] the perfect can be used for situations that hold today without any necessary additional semantic value of current relevance, as in Spanish *lo he visto hoy a las seis de la mañana* 'I saw [literally: have seen] him at six o'clock in the morning today' – note that the English version with the perfect is ungrammatical. In Spanish, then, the one form (perfect) has two meanings: current relevance of a past situation, and recent past. Very often the two will be equivalent informationally (as in most accounts of events that took place earlier on today), but it is possible to distinguish them: the perfect can be used for events that took place much longer ago than today provided they still have current relevance, and the perfect can be used for events that took place earlier on today even if they no longer have current relevance, e.g. *hoy he abierto la ventana a las seis y la he cerrado a las siete* 'today I opened [literally: have opened] the window at six o'clock and closed [literally: have closed] it at seven o'clock', even though the act of opening the window no longer has current relevance.

Before looking at specific examples of degrees of remoteness in tense systems, it will be useful first to outline, in more abstract terms, the possible range of distinctions that can be made in this area, and the parameters that are necessary to a sub-theory of temporal distance as part of a general theory of tense.

Since simultaneity by definition excludes distinctions of temporal distance – if two time points coincide, then one can say nothing other than that they coincide – temporal distance is relevant only with respect to the parameters of 'before' and 'after'. Thus, in principle, one would expect to find distinctions of temporal distance among past tenses and among future tenses. Below, we will see examples of both of these, although it turns out that the more prolific sets of distinctions are more widespread in the past than in the future, in accord with the general tendency of languages to have a better developed past than future system; there are, however, some languages which have symmetrical systems with several oppositions of temporal distance in both past and future.

It is also necessary to specify the reference point from which the temporal distance is measured. For most languages with degrees of remoteness distinctions, it seems that the reference point is taken as the present moment, namely the usual deictic centre for tense systems. There are, however, examples attested where some other deictic centre is necessary. Thus, in Bamileke-Dschang, although the various tenses are normally

---

[2] Information on Limouzi is from Javanaud (1979).

interpreted with absolute time reference,[3] they can be used with relative time reference, at least suggesting that the absolute time reference may be an implicature rather than part of the meaning; at any rate, measurement of temporal distance from a floating reference point is an attested possibility. With absolute-relative tenses, such as the pluperfect, the number of logical possibilities increases exponentially. If a language makes basically, for instance, three distinctions of temporal distance, then this three-way opposition could be applied to the distance between the reference point and the present moment, and to the distance between the situation located and the reference point, giving an opposition of 3^2, i.e. nine terms. We are not aware of any such prolific systems, indeed it seems to be the case that, in languages with absolute-relative tenses and degrees of remoteness, the range of combinations is considerably restricted, often with only oppositions concerning the distance between the situation and the present moment being relevant. In Sotho, however, it is apparently possible to make specific reference to the temporal distance between situation and past reference point in the pluperfect, giving rise to an opposition between *ha letsatsi lelikela rene retsoa tloha Maseru* 'at sunset we had just left Maseru' and *ha letsatsi lelikela rene retlohile Maseru* 'at sunset we had left Maseru', where in our first example our departure from Maseru is located at a short distance in time from the sunset, whereas in the latter it is located further away from that sunset, with no necessary distinction in the temporal distance of the sunset (i.e. the reference point) from the present moment.[4]

Bamileke-Dschang has an even richer system for indicating relative temporal distance. In Bamileke-Dschang, it is possible to have sequences of auxiliaries indicating time reference, though apparently two is the maximum number permitted in sequence. In such a sequence, the first auxiliary establishes time reference relative to the present moment, while the second auxiliary locates the situation relative to the reference point established by the meaning of the first auxiliary. Although not all logically possible combinations are actually allowed by the language, and some combinations receive special interpretations, this still leaves some fifteen combinations which are allowed and given the meanings predictable from the above account. Thus, combination of the tomorrow future (F_3) with the later today future (F_2) indicates a situation that will hold soon after some reference point tomorrow, i.e. 'he will bargain later tomorrow' for *àà 'lùù 'pìŋ'ŋ́ táŋ*; the combination of remote past (P_5) followed by remote future (F_5) indicates a point in time well subsequent to some point in time well

---

[3] Information cited here and below on Bamileke-Dschang is from Hyman (1980).
[4] Information cited here and below on Sotho is from Morolong (1978).

into the past, as in *à lè lá? nfú ńtáŋ* 'he long ago bargained a long time afterwards'.

A third parameter is the number of distinctions made with regard to temporal distance. The most common systems make a small number of distinctions, often two or three, but, as will be seen below, there are languages with more prolific systems: five-way oppositions are attested from Africa, Australia, and the Americas, while one Amerindian language, Kiksht, has been claimed as having a system of around seven oppositions.[5] Temporal distance oppositions are, as already noted, more frequent in the past than in the future, so that Haya, for instance, has a three-way distinction in the past but only a two-way distinction in the future, although there are also languages like Bamileke-Dschang and Bamileke-Ngyemboon with symmetrical systems of, respectively, five and four degrees of remoteness in both past and future.[6] It should be noted that even closely related languages, even dialects of the same language, can differ on this parameter, as in the different number of such tenses in Bamileke-Dschang and Bamileke-Ngyemboon, the different number of tenses in Haya and Luganda (closely related Bantu languages), the rich tense system of Kiksht versus the paucity of tenses in other forms of Chinookan, and between the Mabuiag and Saibai dialects of Kalaw Lagaw Ya (the latter lacks a correspondent to the 'last night' tense of Mabuiag)[7] – for details, see below.

In relation to the number of distinctions, it is also necessary to specify precisely what the cut-off points are for the various distinctions, e.g. a distinction between 'recently' and 'longer ago', or between 'today' and 'earlier today', or a distinction between 'this year' and 'before this year', etc. It turns out that only a very small number of such cut-off points are used with any frequency across the languages of the world with grammaticalisation of temporal distance. The commonest cut-off point seems to be that between 'today' and 'before today', to which we can give the Latinate names hodiernal and pre-hodiernal. Another common cut-off point is that between 'recently' and 'not recently', i.e. between recent and non-recent. For languages with more distinctions in the past, a cut-off point between 'yesterday' and 'before yesterday' is common, but apparently only in conjunction with a cut-off point between 'today' and 'yesterday'; we might

---

[5] Information cited here and below on Kiksht is from Hymes (1975).

[6] Information cited here and below on Haya is from unpublished work by Ernest R. Byarushengo; information on Bamileke-Ngyemboon, except where otherwise stated, is from Anderson (1983).

[7] Information cited here and below on Kalaw Lagaw Ya is, for the Mabuiag dialect, from Bani & Klokeid (1972), and for the Saibai dialect from my own notes supplemented by discussion with Rod Kennedy.

refer to the terms distinguished by the former cut-off point by the Latinate names hesternal and pre-hesternal. Another cut-off point found recurrently in the past is between 'a few days ago' and 'more than a few days ago', i.e. non-remote versus remote. Other cut-off points seem to be language specific. Thus the Mabuiag dialect of Kalaw Lagaw Ya has a special tense for 'last night'. Distinctions with cut-off points prior to 'a few days ago' are also found: one especially prolific system is that of Kiksht, where in addition to cut-off points based on the change of days (e.g. 'today' versus 'yesterday'), there are also cut-off points based on the change of years (e.g. 'this year' versus 'before this year'); but so far, this example stands unique. The range of distinctions made in the future is similar, with the distinction between 'today-tomorrow' versus 'after tomorrow' being particularly common, in addition to distinctions between 'immediate future' and 'non-immediate future' and between 'next few days' versus 'after the next few days'.

It will be noted that many of the cut-off points refer to cyclically recurring changes, such as the succession of days, and one might therefore wonder, in the light of the discussion in section 1.5, whether this might introduce notions of cyclic time reference. For a few languages, cyclicity does seem to be introduced in such instances, in the following way. The examples are from Burera, although similar systems have been reported for a few other Australian Aboriginal languages, and the tense system of Kiksht works in a similar, though more prolific, way.[8] Burera has a two-way formal opposition, namely one tense with the suffix *-nga* (for one class of verbs), and another with the suffix *-de* for this class of verbs, which includes *ngupa-* 'eat', i.e. *ngupa-nga* versus *ngupa-de*. The form *ngupa-nga* can mean either 'I am eating', i.e. present time reference, or 'I ate within the past few days (but excluding today)'; the time reference of this form is thus discontinuous, since it can be used for ongoing situations or for situations that happened before today but within the last few days; it cannot be used for situations holding earlier on today. The time reference of *ngupa-de* is likewise discontinuous: it can be used with reference to situations that held earlier on today (i.e. 'I ate today'), and with reference to situations that held more than a few days ago (i.e. 'I ate long ago'). There are thus two

---

[8] The Burera material is presented by Glasgow (1964); cf. also the discussion of frames of reference for temporal adverbials in Australian languages by Dixon (1977: 498–500). Although Hyman (1980: 235) uses a feature [±NEAR] for the Bamileke-Dschang tense system which gives rise to discontinuities – if the past tenses are numbered 1 to 4 from most to least recent, P1 and P3 are both [+NEAR], distinguished thereby from P2 and P4 respectively, which are [−NEAR], he does not give any reason (other than the elegance of binary features) for grouping P1 and P3 together versus P2 and P4.

remarkable features of this system: each of the two tenses has discontinuous time reference (contrary to the universal posited in section 2.4); the two alternate cyclically, with *ngupa-nga* for the present moment, *ngupa-de* for situations earlier on today, then *ngupa-nga* again for situations up to a few days ago, then *ngupa-de* again for situations in the more distant past. This can be analysed by assuming that Burera has a basic distinction between 'close' and 'remote' which is superimposed on a cut-off point between 'today' and 'earlier than today'. *Ngupa-nga* is the close tense, and within the 'today' frame receives present time reference, while within the 'not today' frame it receives an interpretation as the most recent time period that is not today, i.e. the last few days. Similarly, *ngupa-de* is remote; within the 'today' time frame it receives the interpretation 'as remote as possible but still today', i.e. at some time other than the present moment today, while within the 'not today' frame it receives the interpretation 'remote and not today' i.e. more than a few days ago. The cyclicity thus arises from the combination of two oppositions, one an absolute cut-off point between today and earlier than today, the other between recent and remote within each of these two time frames. This kind of tense opposition does not fit well within most current conceptions of tense, although its existence must be acknowledged; at best, one could appeal to its rarity as an excuse for according it marginal status within the overall theory.

Although we have so far referred to cut-off points, we have not yet indicated how rigidly these cut-off points are to be interpreted – certainly, some of the suggested distinctions (e.g. between 'a few days ago' and 'more than a few days ago') are relatively vague. In fact, there are two problems involved here. One is the precise establishment of the cut-off point. While a distinction like 'today' versus 'yesterday' might at first seem to be clearcut, it soon turns out that, while there are clear instances of today and clear instances of yesterday, there is also an area in between subject to consider-able cultural and even individual variation, namely the establishment of the precise dividing line between the days. While European technological culture has established an arbitrary cut-off point at midnight, this does not correspond to most people's ordinary language usage in English, where *last night* continues up to the time of waking up in the morning as prelude to the new day, i.e. as far as ordinary usage is concerned the day begins in the morning. In many other cultures, however, the new day begins rather from the preceding sunset, so that the night just past is part of today rather than of yesterday. Where a tense opposition exists correlating with the change of days, it seems that this is simply taken to correspond with the individual's or the culture's conception of the dividing line between the days, and there seems to be no evidence for saying more on this topic with regard to the linguistic reflection of this cut-off point.

What is, however, of linguistic interest is the rigidity with which the cut-off point is interpreted, and here there are clear differences between languages. Thus, in some languages with a hesternal ('yesterday') past tense, that tense must be used for situations that held yesterday and can only be used for situations that held yesterday, thus giving rise to clear ungrammaticality if an inappropriate time adverbial is inserted. In other languages, while the most frequent division is between situations that held yesterday and those that held before yesterday or after yesterday, the dividing line is more fluid, in the sense that a literally inappropriate tense can be used in order to give a subjective impression of greater or smaller temporal distance. Haya, in the past tense series, has rigid cut-off points in this sense. The relevant past tenses, which enter into a three-way opposition, are hodiernal ('earlier on today', e.g. *twákôma* 'we tied up'), hesternal ('yesterday', e.g. *tukomíle*), and remote ('before yesterday', e.g. *túkakôma*). Relevant time adverbials are *mbwéènu* 'today', *nyéígolo* 'yesterday' and *íjo* 'two days ago', and *ijwééli* 'three days ago'.[9] The dividing line between the three tenses is strict, and in particular improper collocations of verb form and time adverbial are rejected outright as ungrammatical. Thus, 'we tied up today' can only be *twákôma mbwéènu*, and not **tukomíle/*túkakôma mbwéènu*; 'we tied up yesterday' can only be *tukomíle nyéígolo*, and not **twákôma/*túkakôma mbwéènu*; 'we tied up the day before yesterday' can only be *tukakom' ijo*, and not **twákôm'/*tukomíle íjo*. Although the uses of the verb forms are illustrated here using collocation with adverbials, it should be noted that the constraints are not simply on collocation with adverbials: even if there is no adverbial present, it is impossible in Haya to use the hodiernal past tense to refer to yesterday's situation, and similarly for other combinations.

In Sotho, however, it seems possible in principle to combine any past tense with any past time adverbial without giving rise to ungrammaticality, since distinctions of temporal distance are subjective rather than objective. An apparently incorrect combination will be interpreted to mean that the situation in question, though objectively at a certain temporal distance from the reference point, is being presented as subjectively closer or more distant than that literal distance. Thus, in Sotho we have sentences like *Morena*

---

[9] The adverbs *íjo* and *ijwééli* can also refer to, respectively, 'two days from today' and 'three days from today', i.e. have both past and future time reference. This does not apply to *nyéígolo*, which contrasts with *nyéńkya* 'tomorrow'. In the verb forms, *tu-* (*tw-* before a vowel) is the first person plural subject prefix, while *kom-* is the verb stem 'tie'.

Moshoeshoe ofalletse Thaba Bosiu ka-1824 'Chief Moshoeshoe moved to Thaba-Bosiu in 1824' with a recent past tense, the speaker's intention being to emphasise the subjective recency of the situation, even though the adverbial objectively situates the situation in the distant past. Similarly in Bamileke-Dschang, one would expect the time adverbial *è'zɔɔ* 'tomorrow' to co-occur with the verb form *àà 'lù'ú* (or: *'sù?'é) táŋ* 'he will bargain tomorrow', i.e. the verb form that is normally used for situations holding tomorrow, but it is also possible to use the tense normally meaning 'within the next few days after tomorrow', as in *à'á lá? 'táŋ é'zɔɔ*, with the implication that subjectively the time of his bargaining is further into the future than would be indicated by the objective designation 'tomorrow'. Conversely, one can use the 'tomorrow' past tense with the adverbial *àlé? zèé* 'day after tomorrow' to indicate the subjective closeness of an objectively more distant situation, as in *àà 'lù'ú táŋ àlé? zèé* 'he will bargain (already) the day after tomorrow'. It should be noted that in languages with such fluid boundaries between tenses expressing different degrees of remoteness, it is not just the case that the speaker is playing with extended meanings of items, as when in English one talks of *the movie stars of yesterday* referring to a time more distant than literally *yesterday*: in these Sotho and Bamileke-Dschang examples, the time adverbials continue to be used in their literal meanings, so there is no metaphorical extension – rather the difference between these languages on the one hand and Haya on the other indicates that languages differ on the parameter of the rigidness of interpretation of temporal distance boundaries in tense systems.

Finally, it should be noted that even closely related languages may differ in the rigidity with which temporal distance cut-off points are interpreted (and it is possible that further investigation may even uncover idiolectal distinctions). As already noted, in Bamileke-Dschang the cut-off points are not interpreted rigidly; in the closely-related and mutually intelligible Bamileke-Ngyemboon, however, they are so interpreted, so that the combinations of tense and time adverbial discussed in the previous paragraph would not be possible in Ngyemboon.[10]

Before looking at specific tense systems distinguishing degrees of remoteness, it is worth examining a possibility that arises from the existence of recent past and immediate future cut-off points. This is the possibility that there may be languages where the basic pivot of the tense system is not the present moment, but rather some such recent past or immediate future pivot, so that there would be a basic tense opposition between, say distant past and everything else, or between distant future and everything else. For

---

[10] Stephen C. Anderson (personal communication).

one language, essentially this claim has been made, namely for Nenets, although the data are not sufficiently detailed to permit an exact assessment.[11] In Nenets, for the non-future there are two categories, often called present and past, but perhaps more accurately referred to as indefinite and past. The past is used with past time reference, but only for more distant past situations. For more recent situations, as for ongoing situations, the indefinite is used; thus it is quite possible for the indefinite *tim? xadav* to mean 'I killed a reindeer', where *xadav* is the first person singular of the indefinite tense. Somewhat similar groupings of recent past with present are found in some other languages. Thus, in Bamileke-Ngyemboon, the so-called present tense has an imperfective/perfective aspectual distinction. The present imperfective indicates an ongoing action, but the present perfective is used specifically to indicate a recent past situation.[12] Similar aspectual oppositions between present and recent past are noted for Kom and Noni.[13] In the West African languages cited, for which the data are much more reliable in their detail than for Nenets, this seems to be the maximal utilisation of the intersection of tense and aspect: since the imperfective aspect is rarely needed for recent past situations, and the perfective aspect is rarely needed for currently ongoing situations, the assignment of the appropriate time relation difference to the aspectual opposition gains maximum economy while not violating the basic meaning of the aspectual opposition. It may even be academic whether the tense that overlaps recent past and present is called present or recent past, or a combination of the two.[14]

A more puzzling relevance of recent past and immediate future cut-off points is found in Kalaw Lagaw Ya.[15] Here there is one tense that is used to refer to 'events that have just been completed or that are going on at present', and another that is used to refer to 'events in the immediate future, and often events going on right now'. Both tenses are compatible with the adverbial *kedha thonara* 'at this time', and there is no separate present tense in addition to these two. Thus it seems that one tense covers recent past and present, while the other covers present and immediate future, with overlap between them. One possible interpretation of this is that the first of these tenses indicates present relevance of a (recent) past situation, while the second indicates present relevance of an (immediate) future situation, with

---

[11] Tereščenko (1965: 895–896).

[12] Anderson (1983).

[13] Hyman (1980: 235–236).

[14] Cf. the different solutions suggested by Hyman (1980: 235–236) and Anderson (1983).

[15] Bani & Klokeid (1972: 100–101); their examples, and those cited below, are from the Mabuiag dialect, but the Saibai system is identical on this score.

present time reference being essentially an implicature: thus the first tense would be used with present time reference where the current situation is the result of some previous event, while the second tense would be used rather where the current situation is leading up to some future event.[16] It is possible that the Nenets indefinite tense should be interpreted in a way similar to the interpretation suggested for the Kalaw Lagaw Ya recent past/ present. Kalaw Lagaw Ya examples are *ngau umai ngaikia thoeidhi* (recent past/present) *kedha thonara* 'my dog has bitten me at this time'; *ngath nin iman* (recent past/present) *kedha thonara uuzi pagan* (recent past/present) 'I see you at this time spearing a stonefish'; *senub gulaigau ubiginga Mabuigika pathaika kasa kedha nui pathika* (present/immediate future) *kedha thonara* 'this captain didn't want to go to Mabuiag, but he is going at this time'; *ngath nin imaik* (present/immediate future) *kedha thonara uuzi pagaik* (present/immediate future) 'I'll watch you at this time spearing a stonefish'.

We may now turn to an examination of the temporal distance systems that various languages have, rather than just looking at the isolated parameters that can be combined to make up such systems. In most languages with oppositions of temporal distance in the past, one of the cut-off points is between today and yesterday (with eventual modifications for more and less fluid cut-off points, as discussed above). This dividing line is found, for instance, in the Romance languages that have a near/remote past tense distinction. For French, this distinction apparently held in the seventeenth century,[17] although in the modern language the tendency for the compound past to oust the simple past has led to loss of this distinction: thus, in modern French there is no temporal distance difference between *j'ai écrit* and *j'écrivis* 'I wrote', while in seventeenth-century French the former would have indicated a less remote situation than the latter, as in the contrast between *j'ai écrit ce matin* 'I wrote [literally: have written] this morning' and *j'écrivis hier* 'I wrote yesterday'. Although this distinction of temporal remoteness no longer survives in French, it does survive in (some) Occitanian dialects, such as Limouzi, as with recent *i m'an letsa* (literally: 'they me have released'), remote *i me latseren* 'they released me'. This same cut-off point is found in the binary past tense system of Luganda, e.g. *abagenyi baddayo* (hesternal) *ewaabwe jjo ku nkya* 'the visitors returned home yesterday morning', *omulenzi nnamulabye* (hodiernal) *ku nkya* 'I

---

[16] I am grateful to Rod Kennedy for suggesting this interpretation.

[17] Lancelot & Arnauld (1660: 103–104). Incidentally, it seems that the relevant distinction – as with other languages with this distinction – is 'today' versus 'before today', rather than 'within the last twenty-four hours' versus 'more than twenty-four hours ago'.

saw the boy this morning';[18] and in Ancash Quechua, e.g. *Limatam aywarquu* (hodiernal) 'I went to Lima (earlier today)', *Limatam aywarqaa* (pre-hodiernal) 'I went to Lima (before today)'.[19]

The rarer binary opposition in the future also seems characteristically to have a less rigid cut-off point, with the closer future tense often covering today and tomorrow, while the more distant future tense covers all time after tomorrow, but with vacillation in one or both directions across this cut-off point. In section 1.8 we noted that in Haya, where the temporal distance oppositions in the past have rigid cut-off points, there is much more fluidity in the future. It is, however, interesting that the more remote future tense cannot be used to refer to situations that hold later on today or tomorrow, i.e. for 'tomorrow we will go to Katoke' one can say *nyenkyá tulaagyá* (close future) *Katoke*, and not **nyenkyá tuligyá* (remote future) *Katoke*. The close future can, however, be used with any future time reference, but when used for situations holding after tomorrow it indicates subjective nearness: *mwézy' ógulaijá tuligyá* (remote future)/*tulaagyá* (close future) *Katoke* 'next month we will go to Katoke'. It is interesting to note that, to the extent that Haya does have a cut-off point here, that cut-off point is the division between tomorrow and the day after tomorrow, rather than between today and tomorrow, which would have been the mirror image of the usual cut-off point in the past.

Although the division between today and yesterday seems to be the most widespread cut-off point for binary past tense oppositions, and indeed a component of all more prolific systems, there are also some languages in which an opposition exists between recent past, where 'recent' means the immediate past, and non-recent past. Examples are not so clear as with the today/yesterday opposition, and often involve oppositions that are less clearly grammaticalised than those that express the today/yesterday opposition. Thus in French, which does not otherwise distinguish degrees of remoteness in the past, there is a distinct construction for the recent past using the auxiliary *venir* 'to come' and the infinitive of the lexical verb preceded by the preposition *de* 'of, from', as in *je viens d'arriver* 'I have just arrived', literally 'I come from to-arrive'. Likewise, Portuguese uses the auxiliary *acabar* 'to finish' in *acabo de chegar*, literally 'I finish from to-arrive'. (Spanish has the same construction, e.g. *acabo de llegar*, but since Spanish also has today/yesterday as a dividing line in its past tense system, this is not as part of a binary system.) However, use of the special recent past construction is not obligatory, so that in reference to the recent past one can say in French *je suis arrivé*, in Portuguese *cheguei*, just as one can in

[18] Ashton et al. (1951: 122).   [19] Cole (1982: 144).

94

reference to more distant past events. Therefore the identification of these constructions as grammaticalised devices remains questionable. Even in English, the immediate past/more distant past division is relevant in characterising the use of the perfect, which can be used with reference to a small number of time adverbials referring to the immediate past, such as *just* and *recently*. Again, however, this use is optional, and the simple past is equally possible with these adverbials; moreover, the relevant factor is the occurrence of a particular adverbial, rather than recent time reference per se, since a different adverbial, even if expressing immediate past time, does not permit collocation with the perfect, as in **I have seen him a second ago*. Whether the clearly grammatical opposition between indefinite and past tense in Nenets, discussed above, should be included here remains open, awaiting a more detailed discussion and investigation of the Nenets tense system.

Likewise in the future, many languages have constructions with (as part of their meaning) immediate future time reference, but without it being clear that these constructions should be analysed as grammaticalisation of time reference. In English, for instance, the constructions *to be about to* and *to be on the point of* contain immediate future time reference, as in *John is about to jump off the cliff*.[20] However, immediate future time reference does not exhaust the meaning of this construction, which differs from the future not only in range of time reference but also in that it expresses a present propensity to a future situation that may, however, be blocked by intervening factors. Thus *John will jump off the cliff* is untrue if John does not, in fact, jump off the cliff, while *John is about to jump off the cliff* is still true if someone rushes over and prevents him from doing so. For the relevance of an immediate future cut-off point in languages which otherwise lack distinctions of temporal distance in the future, one might compare the discussion in section 1.6 concerning use of the past for immediate future events, as in Russian *ja pošel* 'I'm off', literally 'I left'; these forms, however, are idiomatic rather than grammaticalised.

For three-term systems in the past, the first division is usually between today and yesterday, but the second division is more variable within the time period before today. In Haya, as we have already seen, there is a rigid second division between 'yesterday' and 'before yesterday'. In Hixkaryana, the most recent past tense is used for situations that held earlier on today (including the previous night), e.g. *kahatakano* 'I came out'.[21] The middle term is used for recent events that took place before today, including the previous day but potentially going back up to several months, e.g.

---

[20] Cf. Comrie (1976: 64–65).   [21] Derbyshire (1979: 138–139).

ninikyako 'he went to sleep'. The most remote past tense is described as referring 'to actions done any time earlier', though with the proviso that 'sometimes an event of only a few weeks ago will be expressed with the distant past suffix', e.g. *wamaye* 'I felled it'. Although Kamba is genetically related to Haya (though not particularly closely so within Bantu), the Kamba system is structurally more reminiscent of that of Hixkaryana: the least remote of the three past tenses is used for earlier on today (e.g. *ningootie* 'I pulled'); the middle form is used for time from yesterday back to a week ago (e.g. *ninina:kootie* 'I pulled'); while the third, most remote term, is used typically for actions not earlier than some months previously (e.g. *maia:tūa* 'they did not live').[22] What does, however, seem to be common to clearly grammaticalised three-way systems is that the second division breaks up the time-span before today, rather than the time-span of today. The only potential counterexample I am aware of would be in Spanish, if one takes the *acabar de* construction as indicating immediate past and the perfect as indicating situations that hold earlier on today; however, the optionality of the first of these divisions makes Spanish a much less clear example than the other languages discussed. Note that even Burera, with its strange cyclic tense system, still gives the divisions of the past as earlier on today, within the past few days, before that.

Examples of four-term systems are not particularly frequent, so any generalisation made here is necessarily particularly provisional. One example of a four-term system is Mabuiag, provided one treats the recent past/ present distinction as not being part of the past tense system. If one accepts this analysis, then there is a four-term opposition between a today past (for situations earlier on today), a 'last night' past (for events taking place last night, and thus collocating with the adverbial *kubila* 'at night' to give the interpretation 'last night'), a yesterday past tense, and a more remote past tense. For the verb 'see' the singular forms are, respectively, *imanu, imanbungel, imangul, imadhin* (compare also the recent past/present *iman*). The Saibai dialect of Kalaw Lagaw Ya, incidentally, lacks the 'last night' past tense, giving overall a system more like that of Haya (apart from the complication of the recent past/present tense). Bamileke-Ngyemboon also has a four-term system, though with one complication already discussed: for one tense, the imperfective has present time reference, but the perfective has recent past time reference. In the imperfective there are clearly four distinct past tenses, with time reference: earlier on today; yesterday; within the last few days; a long time ago, e.g. a year or more. In the perfective these same four occur, supplemented by the 'recent past', or

[22] Whiteley & Muli (1962).

perhaps more accurately perfective present. In the future, however, Bamileke-Ngyemboon has unequivocally a four-term opposition, since there is no interaction between aspect and time reference comparable to that found in the past tenses. The forms cited below are 'he cut the meat' in the various tense-aspects (note that there is considerable tone sandhi):

	Perfective	Imperfective
P4	à là lá? nzǎ? mbǎb	à là lá? nzǎ?à mbàb
P3	à là zâ? mbàb	à làa nzǎ? mbàb
P2	à kà zà? mbàb	à kàa nzǎ? mbàb
P1	à ně nzǎ? mbǎb	à kɔ́ nzá?à mbàb
Present	à zǎ? mbǎb	à nzá?à mbàb
F1	à gè zǎ? mbǎb	à gè zǎ?à mbàb
F2	à tɔ́ zǎ? mbǎb	à tɔ́ zǎ?à mbàb
F3	à lù zǎ? mbǎb	à lù zǎ?à mbàb
F4	à lá? zǎ? mbǎb	à lá? zǎ?àmbàb

Five-term systems are also rare, so it is equally difficult to make generalisations likely to stand up to the test of further investigation. The five-term system discussed in most detail in the literature, and for which the discussion is most reliable, is that of Bamileke-Dschang. What is particularly unusual about this language is that it has the five-way opposition in both the past and the future (cf. the almost equally symmetrical system in Bamileke-Ngyemboon). The relevant forms for the verb 'bargain' are as follows; note that for the F3 tense there are two alternative forms:

P1	àá 'táŋ	F1	à'á táŋ
P2	à áà ǹtáŋ	F2	àà 'pìŋ'ŋ́ táŋ
P3	à kè táŋ'ŋ́	F3	àà 'lù'zú táŋ/àà 'šʉ?'é táŋ
P4	à lè táŋ'ŋ́	F4	à'á lá?é 'táŋ
P5	à lè lá? ń'táŋ	F5	à'á fú 'táŋ

The interpretation of numerals is symmetrical: thus the numeral 1 means 'immediate', i.e. P1 is immediate past and F1 is immediate future; the numeral 2 implies 'today', i.e. P2 is used for situations earlier on today and F2 for situations later on today; the numeral 3 implies 'one day from today', i.e. P3 implies 'yesterday' and F3 implies 'tomorrow'; the numeral 4 implies 'within a period from two days to several days from today'; i.e. P4 implies 'the day before yesterday or a few days earlier' and F4 implies 'the day after tomorrow or a few days later'; the numeral 5 indicates further remoteness, e.g. 'separated from today by a year or more', giving P5 'a year or so ago', F5 'a year or more hence'.

Before leaving the Bamileke-Dschang system, it should be noted that most (though not all) of the auxiliaries used in forming this prolific system of tenses also exist as regular verbs in the language. However, although the time reference meaning can often be related to the meaning the corresponding verb has as a separate lexical item, these two sets of meanings are by no means identical, and some sentences are clearly ambiguous according to whether the item in question is interpreted as an auxiliary marking time reference or as a main verb. In fact, the sentence *àà 'lùù 'pìŋ'ŋ́ táŋ* has four quite distinct interpretations. If taken as a sequence of F3 and F2, it will mean 'he will bargain later tomorrow' (cf. p. 86); if the second word is interpreted as a tense auxiliary and the third as a lexical verb, it will mean 'he will return tomorrow and bargain'; if the second word is interpreted as a lexical item and the third as an auxiliary, it will mean 'he is about to get up and later today bargain'; if both are interpreted as lexical items it will mean 'he is about to get up and return and bargain'.[23]

Of the other five-term systems reported in the literature, we may cite that of Yandruwandha, where there is sufficient detail to make it reasonably clear that this is indeed a justified analysis in terms of a five-way tense opposition in the past.[24] The suffixes, with their meanings, are:

-na	very recent past
-ŋana	within the last couple of days
-ŋukarra	within the last few days[25]
-nga	weeks or months ago
-lapurra	distant past

While these characterisations clearly define oppositions in terms of degrees of remoteness – the source cited notes that there is little inconsistency in native speakers' use of these forms in terms of temporal distance, except between *ŋana* and *ŋukara* – more specific information would be required in order to test out some of the hypotheses advanced in the body of this chapter, e.g. whether there is a basic today/yesterday distinction within the system.

For completeness, I will note two five-term systems in the past that have been drawn to my attention from South American Indian languages. Araona is reported to have the following system (although the remarks in

---

[23] Note that the F3 tense auxiliary *lu* redundantly requires the preceding word to be in F1 form; tonal indications are of surface tones, and there are considerable alternations by tone sandhi.

[24] Breen (1976: 755–756).

[25] *ŋukarra* is also a time adverbial.

parentheses suggest that time reference may not be the only relevant parameter):[26]

-iqui	recent past, the same day
-a	recent past, from one day to several weeks ago
-asha	past (from several weeks to several years ago; also may indicate multiple events)
-ana	distant past (possibly also indicates a specific event)
-isa	remote past

Yagua has the following five-term system:[27]

-jásiy	proximate-1 (within a few hours)
-jáy	proximate-2 (one day ago)
-siy	within a few weeks
-tíy	within a few months
-jadá	distant or legendary past

It is interesting that the rich systems of Bamileke-Dschang, Bamileke-Ngyemboon, and Mabuiag on the one hand make fine distinctions relatively close to the present moment, while Yandruwandha, Araona, and Yagua seem to make finer discriminations for more remote events.

Finally, we may consider what is to date the richest reported system of tense distinctions in the past, namely that of Kiksht. Kiksht has basically a four-way opposition in terms of tense prefixes in the past,[28] with *ga(l)-* as the most remote form for events from one year ago back; *ni(g)-* for situations from the preceding week to a year ago; *na(l)-* for situations holding most typically yesterday, but conceivably extending back to the day or a few days before yesterday; and *i(g)-* for situations holding earlier today. However, cross-cutting this five-way distinction is a further two-way distinction, using the prefixes *u-* and *t-*. The time periods defined by the prefixes *ga(l)-*, *ni(g)-*, and perhaps *i(g)-* (but not *na(l)-*), are each subdivided into an earlier portion, marked by the prefix *u-*, and a later portion, marked by the prefix *t-*. This gives overall a six- or seven-way distinction within the past (the uncertainty concerns the possibility of making the *u-/t-* distinction within the *i(g)-* set), as follows:[29]

---

[26] Pitman (1980).

[27] Doris Payne (personal communication).

[28] There is also a prefix *na-*, whose meaning does not, however, seem to be (exclusively) of time reference.

[29] The same formal opposition also occurs in the present, with zero basic tense prefix: the interpretation of the distinction here is more complex (Hymes 1975: 319–321) with at least aspectual overtones, though surprisingly given the usual temporal relation *ó. . .u-* seems to

ga(l) . . . u- remote past
ga(l) . . . t- from one to ten years ago
ni(g) . . . u- from a week to a year ago
ni(g) . . . t- last week
na(l)- yesterday or preceding couple of days
i(g)- earlier today: ʔi(g) . . . u- earlier on today,
but not just now
ʔi(g) . . . t- just now

It is perhaps interesting that this most prolific system results from the intersection of two distinct systems, one the four-term system for indicating remoteness, the other the two-term system for distinguishing earlier and later time, always within one of the time periods defined by the five-term system. Like the Burera system discussed above, the different frames intersecting with the *u-/t-* opposition give rise to a discontinuity in the temporal reference of each of *u-* and *t-*. The *u-/t-* opposition carries into the future, which is not otherwise subdivided for remoteness, giving *a(l)* . . . *u-* (immediate and near future) versus *a(l)* . . . *t-* (distant future); this confirms, incidentally, that the *u-/t-* opposition is one of later versus earlier time (within a given time space), rather than one of remoteness per se, otherwise one would expect the values of the two future tenses to be inverted.

To conclude this chapter, we will examine how the various parameters discussed in the body of the book can be combined in the definition of the temporal reference of one particularly complex form, the perfect in Portuguese. Despite the name 'perfect', the meaning of this form is radically different from that of the English perfect, or the French compound past. The Portuguese perfect indicates a situation that is aspectually habitual (and to this extent falling outside our discussion of tense), that started in the recent past, and that continues up to (but not necessarily including) the present moment. It frequently co-occurs with the adverb *ultimamente* 'recently' and its synonyms. In form, the Portuguese perfect uses the present tense of the auxiliary *ter* 'to have' and the past participle of the lexical verb.[30] Thus the sentence *ele tem estudado muito ultimamente*

indicate present continuous or generic, while *ó. . .t-* indicates 'a time anterior to the present, perhaps with a connotation of continuation into, or continued relevance to [the present]'.

[30] Note that the Portuguese perfect, though formally part of the same system as the compound pluperfect (*tinha estudado* 'he has studied'), stands functionally outside this system. Even the formally corresponding subjunctive (*tenha estudado*) does not have the usual semantics of the perfect indicative *tem estudado*.

indicates that he started studying in the not too distant past, established a habit of studying, and that this habit has continued up to the present moment – although it may be that the habit has now come to an end, just before the present moment.[31] Thus the time reference of the Portuguese perfect is past; we need to identify a point in time in the not too distant past (the verb form does not further specify which point in time), and a point in time infinitesimally prior to the present moment; the time reference of the Portuguese perfect then covers the whole span from one of these time points to the other.

[31] If it is desired to indicate explicitly that the habit does include the present moment, then Portuguese requires use of the present tense, i.e. *ele estuda muito ultimamente*. Both the sentence in the text and the sentence just cited translate most naturally into English as 'he has been studying a lot recently', but it is important to notice that this is a translation equivalent rather than an analysis – the two Portuguese sentences differ in meaning, albeit slightly. The version with the perfect does not include extension of the situation described to the present moment, although equally it does not explicitly exclude extension to the present moment; the version with the present tense explicitly extends the situation to the present moment.

5
Tense and syntax

At various points in the discussion so far, and especially in chapter 1, we have mentioned in passing that apparent exceptions to the use of a given tense as defined by its meaning can be accounted for in terms of the interaction of the meaning of that tense with independently justifiable syntactic rules of the language in question. To justify this position, of course, it is necessary to specify what these syntactic rules are, and to show how their interaction with the meanings of tenses does indeed give rise to the observed apparent anomalies in tense usage. In this chapter, we shall look in greater detail at some examples of this interaction, to illustrate the way in which such apparent anomalies should be handled within an integrated approach to the description of a language. The interplay between the semantics of tense and syntax in fact predicts that the observed apparent anomalies in tense usage should occur; if they did not, it would be necessary to revise the theory. That is why such anomalies are referred to as apparent anomalies: the independently justified meaning of a tense interacts with an independently justifiable syntactic principle in order to produce a use of the tense which, superficially, seems to contradict the meaning of that tense.

5.1 Tense neutralisation

In several languages, there is a rule whereby within what would otherwise be a sequence of like tenses within a sentence, only the first verb shows the expected tense, while all subsequent verbs are in a single tense category, irrespective of the tense of the first verb (and thus the time reference of the later verbs). This may be compared with the way in which other categories may be neutralised if they would take identical values across a series of clauses within a single sentence, as when in English *I must go out and buy some bread* the debitive (obligative) modality is expressed overtly in the first clause by *must* which then carries across, without overt expression, to the second clause, i.e. the interpretation is that *I must buy some bread.*

In Bahinemo, the neutralised tense verb forms in question have overtly the form of the present, as in the following example, where the first verb is in the remote past tense, all following verbs in the present:[1]

Nem   na   ya-tagiya-m,   du-qi-yasinu,
we   sago eat-satisfy-remote:past   neutral-repeat-get:up:present

de-tenowa-u,   niba   la-hina-fanel,
neutral-ascend-present   ridge immediate-upstream-arrive:present

idu   du-wei
to:right   neutral-walk:along:ridge:present

'After we ate sago until we were satisfied, we got up again, we ascended, immediately we went up the stream bed and arrived at the ridge, we walked along the ridge to the right.'

A similar situation has been reconstructed for Proto-Indo-European, for the so-called injunctive, although the attested data from early Indo-European languages, such as Vedic Sanskrit, are not as clear-cut as those from Bahinemo above.[2] In the reconstructed system, however, the so-called augment, Proto-Indo-European *e-*, indicates past time reference, cf. Ancient Greek *e-lý-omen* 'we used to free', i.e. 'past free first:plural'. In a sequence of past time reference verbs, however, the past time reference is marked overtly only on the first of these verbs, i.e. this verb takes the augment but following verbs are in the same form but lacking the augment (the so-called injunctive); thus these following verbs are not explicitly marked for past time reference. This would then give a situation similar to that outlined above for Bahinemo, where tense is marked overtly only on the first verb in a sequence of verbs with like time reference.

It is important, in order to avoid confusion, to clarify exactly what the similarity is between the verbs in sequence that permits tense neutralisation to take place. At first sight, one might think that the only relevant consideration is identity of tense. However, it seems not to be possible to have constructions with tense neutralisation where the tenses of all verbs would be the same (if, for instance, the discourse were presented as a series of independent sentences, rather than as a single whole), but where their actual time references are radically different, for instance with one situation holding a considerable period before another. Thus more accurately one

---

[1] Longacre (1972: 47–48).
[2] Kiparsky (1968).

should say that the verbs in question must have the same time reference for this neutralisation to be possible. This might seem to be in conflict with the chronological sequencing that normally forms part of the interpretation of such a construction, as in the Bahinemo example cited: strictly, the verbs do not have the same time reference, since the events in question happen in sequence, rather than simultaneously. However, if we bear in mind that narration of an event establishes a covert reference point corresponding to the end of that event, such that the next event narrated can freely be interpreted as starting at the completion of the previously narrated event, then the problem disappears: the time reference of a tense-neutralised verb is that established by the immediately preceding sentence-internal context.

The above discussion enables us to solve two apparent problems in tense semantics. First, there is the problem (as in Bahinemo) that one tense, the present, has some uses that apparently contradict its meaning of present time reference; the rule neutralising tenses in sequence to the present provides a syntactic principle which accounts for this apparent anomaly. Secondly, we can give a characterisation to categories that apparently have no tense value, such as the Proto-Indo-European injunctive: its time reference is simply location at the time established by the immediately preceding sentence-internal context; the requirement that there be a preceding sentence-internal context excludes this category from occurring sentence-initially.

5.2 Sequence of tenses

In Fula, there is a rule very similar to that operating in Bahinemo and Proto-Indo-European, whereby tense is neutralised in a sequence.[3] However, in Fula there are two distinct sets of verb forms that can occur in the position of neutralisation, the so-called relative past and the subjunctive. The distribution of these two forms in such sequences is determined entirely by the syntax: if the initial verb is one of the past tenses, then the neutralised verbs stand in the relative past; if the initial verb is a non-past tense, then the neutralised verb stands in the subjunctive, as in the following examples: *teema 'o-nan* (emphatic past) *sonnyo mab'b'e, 'o-wari* (relative past) *ndaaruki b'e* 'perhaps he heard the:sound of-them, he came to:look:at them'; *jaŋŋgo mi yahay* (general future), *mi-foonda-ki* (subjunctive), *mi-ndaara* (subjunctive) 'tomorrow I will:go, I will:test it, I will:see'. In Fula, then, we see operating exactly the same process as in Bahinemo, but superimposed on this process is a syntactic rule of sequence

---

[3] Arnott (1970: 326–332). The data are from the Gombe dialect (northern Nigeria). I have replaced Arnott's special symbols for the implosives by *b'* and *d'*.

of tenses, which requires different neutralised tenses depending on the tense of the initial verb. In these examples, it would be misleading to argue for a difference in time reference between the relative past and the subjunctive in tense-neutralised environments. Rather, they have the same time reference – location in time at the time point identified by the immediately preceding sentence-internal context – the difference between them being conditioned by a purely syntactic rule.

Turning to a different construction, namely indirect commands (i.e. commands expressed in indirect speech), we find a similar rule of sequence of tense in a number of European languages. In an indirect command, such as *I told John to go away* or *I will tell John to go away*, the time reference of the verb contained within the command (i.e. *go* in these examples) is invariably future relative to the time reference of the main verb. (It is not always possible to determine its absolute time reference: thus, in the first example, my intention may have been that John should have gone before the present moment – or I may even have intended to leave it quite open when he should go away, relative to the present moment.) Thus, in general, there can be no contrast in tense expressing a contrast in time reference in this position,⁴ and indeed English uses just one form here, the infinitive, irrespective of the tense of the main verb.

In some other languages, however, the tense of the verb expressing the content of the command does vary, not, however, in terms of its own independent time reference, but on the basis of a syntactic rule of sequence of tenses. Thus, in Spanish, the content of an indirect command is normally expressed by a clause with its verb in the subjunctive mood, the past subjunctive being used if the main verb is in one of the past tenses, and the present subjunctive if the main verb is in one of the non-past tenses, as in the following examples:⁵ *dije que Juan se fuese* (past subjunctive) 'I told Juan

---

⁴ In a language which makes grammatical distinctions of degrees of remoteness, there could be a tense distinction depending on the elapsed time between the moment of my issuing the instruction and the moment at which I want John to carry it out. In languages with relative tense distinctions, there could be a relative tense distinction relating to some reference point other than of the command, as in English *I told John to have finished his homework before I returned*, where John's finishing his homework is located anterior to my returning, though still subsequent to the time of my issuing the instruction. Some speakers of English marginally allow sentences like *I told John not to have worked in vain*, with the interpretation 'I told John not to do anything that would render his previous work in vain', where John's work is no doubt prior to the moment at which the instruction is issued, but the evaluation of whether or not it is in vain can only be subsequent.

⁵ Note, however, that from the use of the subjunctive in other constructions one can isolate past versus non-past time reference as being part of the meaning of these subjunctive forms in the absence of sequence of tenses, as for instance when used with the adverb *quizás* 'perhaps' to indicate a situation which is possible but, in the speaker's estimation, unlikely:

to go away', literally 'I-said that Juan go-away', *digo (siempre) que Juan se vaya* (present subjunctive) 'I (always) tell Juan to go away', *diré/voy a decir que Juan se vaya* 'I will tell Juan to go away'. It makes no sense to ask about the difference in time reference between the present and past subjunctive here. Indeed, it is even conceivable that they could have the same time reference, as in the following pair of examples: *dije que Juan se fuese mañana* 'I told Juan to leave tomorrow', *voy a decir que Juan se vaya mañana* 'I will tell Juan to leave tomorrow': the time reference of Juan's leaving is tomorrow in both sentences, what is different is the time at which I issue the instruction, and this, coupled with the sequence of tenses rule, conditions the different tenses of the subjunctive. Thus we conclude that the only way in which the different uses of the two tenses of the subjunctive can be accounted for in indirect commands is by a rule of sequence of tenses, which overrides other considerations of time reference.

There is one slight complication to the rule of sequence for tenses in Spanish, which will be treated here not only for completeness but also because similar phenomena arise in the discussion of indirect speech in section 5.3. Even where the main verb is in a past tense, it is possible (though not obligatory) to use the present subjunctive provided the command issued still has validity, i.e. provided it can still be complied with. This can be seen by contrasting the following two situations. In the first situation, I issued an instruction to Juan yesterday that he should leave yesterday. In other words, for Juan to comply with this instruction, he would have had to leave yesterday; leaving today is not sufficient, because the instruction clearly no longer has validity. In this situation in Spanish, only the past subjunctive is possible: *dije que Juan se fuese ayer* 'I told Juan to leave yesterday'. Suppose, however, that although I issued the order to Juan yesterday, it related to his departure tomorrow (i.e. two days after I issued the order, and one day after the present moment). In this case, at the present moment the order still has validity, and in Spanish one can say either *dije que Juan se fuese mañana*, using the past subjunctive as by the sequence of tenses rule, or *dije que Juan se vaya mañana*, using the present subjunctive as the instruction still has validity.

In this latter situation, where the instruction still has validity, it would also be possible to use the perfect in place of the preterite in the main clause, to make explicit the continuing relevance of the instruction *he dicho que Juan se vaya mañana* 'I have told Juan to leave tomorrow', though for some speakers of Spanish this is not possible if the main clause contains an

Juan esté (present) *quizás en Los Ángeles* 'Juan is perhaps in Los Angeles', *Juan estuviese* (past) *quizás en Los Ángeles* 'Juan was perhaps in Los Angeles'.

adverb referring to a past time prior to today, i.e. not all speakers of Spanish accept *he dicho ayer que Juan se fuese/vaya mañana.* (In English, the literal translation 'I have told Juan yesterday to leave tomorrow' is, of course, ungrammatical because of the general restriction in English against collocating the perfect with adverbials referring to a specific time in the past.) This last judgement makes it clear that what is relevant in the examples of this paragraph is not the tense of the verb in the main clause as such, but rather the continuing validity of the instruction.[6] Thus we may summarise the Spanish sequence of tenses rule in indirect commands as follows: past subjunctive after a main verb in the past tense, except that where the content of the subordinate clause has continuing validity the present subjunctive may be used; otherwise, present subjunctive. We shall now see that a very similar rule, interacting in interesting ways with tense meanings, exists in English for indirect speech.

5.3 Indirect speech in English and Russian

The purpose of this section is to illustrate further sequence of tenses by means of a detailed consideration of one particular construction, namely indirect speech in English. Since the rules for indirect speech in Russian are different from those in English, as far as the use of tenses is concerned, Russian data have been included to provide contrast with the English material. To provide for easy comparability and to keep the discussion within manageable proportions, it is restricted to examples of indirect statements after the main verb *say* (Russian imperfective *govorit'*, perfective *skazat'*).

In both English and Russian, there is a clear distinction between direct and indirect speech.[7] In direct speech, the original speaker's exact words are

[6] In Latin the perfect, which covers the semantic range of both the Spanish preterite and the perfect, can belong either to 'primary sequence', i.e. take a following present subjunctive, or to 'secondary (historic) sequence', i.e. take a following past subjunctive, according to the same principles as described for Spanish. While this might seem to be a criterion for treating the Latin perfect as the superficial syncretisation of two distinct underlying verb categories, say 'perfect' and 'preterite', the discussion in the text demonstrates that this is not necessary: the difference between primary and secondary sequences can be handled in terms of the interpretations of sentences without the need to invoke distinct covert categories. Moreover, the fact that in Spanish, which has a distinction between perfect and preterite, the distinction between primary and secondary sequences does not correspond necessarily to that between perfect and preterite in the main clause suggests that even less motivation exists for the covert opposition analysis of the Latin data.

[7] Some languages lack a clear-cut distinction between direct and indirect speech, but what is crucial for our present purposes, where indirect speech serves only as an illustration of the interaction of tense meanings and syntactic rules, is that English and Russian do have such a distinction. In English there is, incidentally, one set of adverbials that seems to behave

reproduced, without any change whatsoever, as in *John said yesterday, 'I shall leave tomorrow'*. Note in particular that in this example the pronoun *I* refers to the original speaker, i.e. John; the adverb *tomorrow* is interpreted from the viewpoint of the original speaker's deictic centre, i.e. the time reference of *tomorrow* is the day after John's utterance. In indirect speech, two obvious changes take place. The first, which is optional, is that the speaker's original wording may be changed, as long as the same content is expressed as in the original utterance; in the example above one might, for instance, replace *leave* by *depart*, as in *John said that he would depart today*.

More important for present purposes is the shift in deictic centre, although for the moment we will specifically exclude tense from our discussion. Apart from tense, all the other elements sensitive in the speaker's original utterance to his deictic centre are shifted to correspond to the deictic centre of the person reporting this utterance. Thus, in the example above, in indirect speech we find *he* for *I* of the original, and *today* for *tomorrow* of the original. It is important to note that what is relevant in going from direct to indirect speech is the shift in deictic centre, and not any mechanical procedure for replacing one set of forms by another. Thus, imagine that John says to Mary: *you are intelligent*. Now, if I report this to Harry I will replace *you* by *she*, to give *John said to Mary that she was intelligent*. If, however, I report this back to Mary, then *you* will remain unchanged: *John said to you that you were intelligent*. If Mary reports this to me, then *you* will be replaced by *I*: *John said to me that I was intelligent*. What these examples show is that any attempt to set up a mechanical procedure for changing pronouns and adverbials in indirect speech would require so many conditions that it would be hopelessly cumbersome; whereas the simple instruction to change the deictic centre automatically produces the required deictics.

In Russian, the same shift in deictics takes place in indirect speech. Thus, if John's original words yesterday were *ja ujda zavtra* 'I will leave tomorrow', then I can report this by saying *Džon skazal, čto on ujdet*

anomalously with respect to the shift in deictic centre in indirect speech, namely adverbials with *ago*. Outside indirect speech, an expression like *ten years ago* invariably takes the here-and-now as deictic centre, and cannot be used with reference to any other deictic centre; cf. *I arrived here ten years ago*, but *I left that city last year, having arrived there ten years before/ earlier*, where the ten years are to be counted from my leaving that city, not from the present moment. In indirect speech, however, one can have *John said that he had arrived ten years ago*, which allows both the interpretation where the ten years are counted from the here-and-now and the interpretation where the ten years are counted from the time of John's utterance.

segodnja 'John said that he would leave [literally: will leave] today'. A simpler example, in which the deictic of the reported speech changes from a shifter (absolute time reference) to a connector (relative time reference) is illustrated by the following Russian examples with their English versions: *Džon skazal: 'Ja ujdu zavtra'*; *John said, 'I will leave tomorrow'*; *Džon skazal, čto on ujdet na sledujuščij den'* ; *John said that he would leave on the following day*. There is, however, one crucial difference between English and Russian indirect speech, and this concerns precisely the tense of the verb in the indirect speech. In Russian, the verb in indirect speech remains in the same tense as in the corresponding direct speech, i.e. there is no shift whatsoever. This means that tenses in indirect speech in Russian are interpreted not from the viewpoint of the deictic centre of the here-and-now, but rather with the deictic centre of the original speaker. This therefore contrasts with the shift in the deictic centre for all other deictics in Russian, as also in English.

In English, clearly there is a (possible) change in the tense of the verb in the shift from direct to indirect speech, as we can see in the replacement of *will leave* (with future time reference) by *would leave* in the examples just cited. At first sight, it might seem that this follows from the general change of deictic centre already observed for other deictics. With this particular example, this would indeed be compatible with the meaning of the future in the past (conditional) *would leave*: a reference point is established in the past (namely, the time of John's utterance), and the time reference of the situation located (i.e. John's departure) is subsequent to this reference point. Below, however, we shall see that this is not the correct analysis of tense in indirect speech in English, since there is a different analysis which gives correct predictions in a number of instances where the shift of deictic centre analysis gives the wrong prediction for use of tense in indirect speech; it just happens that in the example discussed both analyses give the same prediction.

Before leaving the Russian example, it should be noted that the interaction of the rule requiring shift of deictics other than tense and the absence of any shift in tense, between direct and indirect speech, can lead to apparent conflicts between time reference of the verb and of adverbials. (As we shall see below, similar conflicts can arise in English, so further discussion of the Russian data is appropriate for comparative purposes even in the context of discussing the English material.) Let us imagine that today is the fifteenth of May. In our first scenario, Kolya uttered the following on the eighth of May: *ja pridu četyrnadcatogo maja* 'I will arrive on the fourteenth of May'. If I report this today in Russian, then I will say *Kolja skazal, čto on pridet četyrnadcatogo maja* 'Kolya said that he would arrive [literally: will arrive] on the fourteenth of May'. The tense in this sentence is future *pridet*, although from the deictic centre of the reporter it has past time reference, given its collocation with the adverbial *četyrnadcatogo maja*, which has past time reference. This Russian example is fully acceptable.

Similarly, if one takes a second scenario where Kolya's utterance is in the future, i.e. on the twentieth of May he will claim to have arrived on the sixteenth of May, Kolya's actual words will then be *ja prišel šestnadcatogo maja* 'I arrived on the sixteenth of May'. If I report this claim today, then the form will be: *Kolja skažet, čto on prišel šestnadcatogo maja* 'Kolya will say that he arrived on the sixteenth of May'. Here the tense of *prišel* is past, although relative to the reporter's deictic centre it has future time reference, as is clear from the adverbial *šestnadcatogo maja*, which has future time reference. Thus it is possible in Russian to combine past tense with future time reference and future tense with past time reference, and indeed these combinations are predicted by the generalisation that says that tense is not changed in moving from direct to indirect speech.

Of course, if today is the fifteenth of May, then it would be possible to refer to the fourteenth of May simply as *yesterday*, Russian *včera*, and to the sixteenth of May as *tomorrow*, Russian *zavtra*. Thus we might expect to be able to rephrase the above Russian sentences with indirect speech as follows: **Kolja skazal, čto on pridet včera* 'Kolya said that he would arrive yesterday', **Kolja skažet, čto on prišel zavtra* 'Kolya will say that he arrived tomorrow'. For at least a wide range of Russian speakers, these two sentences are ungrammatical, even though the principles outlined so far would suggest that they should be fully grammatical, with the meanings and interpretations intended.[8] It seems therefore that Russian (or at least, Russian for many of its speakers, should it turn out that there is variation in judgements on such examples) has a constraint preventing collocation of a given tense with an adverbial whose meaning is incompatible with the meaning of that tense. Thus it is impossible to collocate the past tense (which has past time reference as its meaning) with *zavtra* 'tomorrow', because the meaning of *zavtra* ('day after today') includes future time reference and is thus incompatible with past time reference. Likewise, it is impossible to collocate *pridet* (future tense, future time reference as its meaning) with *včera* 'yesterday', since the meaning of *včera* ('day before today') is incompatible with future time reference. The unacceptability of

---

[8] For some English-speakers with whom I have consulted, the gloss to the second Russian sentence is unacceptable (i.e. *Kolya will say that he arrived tomorrow*), although the gloss to the first sentence is acceptable to all speakers. I return to this point below.

the examples discussed in this paragraph, in contrast to the acceptability of the examples discussed in the previous two paragraphs, is, incidentally, strong evidence for the need to distinguish between meaning and interpretation, not least in the discussion of tense and time reference. The verb form *pridet* (future tense) in **Kolja skazal, čto on pridet včera* 'Kolya said that he would arrive yesterday' has past time reference, but what is crucial for the rule restricting collocations of adverbials and tenses is not the actual time reference, but rather the meaning of this grammatical category, which is: future time reference. In the informationally equivalent *Kolja skazal, čto on pridet četyrnadcatogo maja* 'Kolya said that he would arrive on the fourteenth of May', there is no violation of this collocation restriction: although the adverbial *četyrnadcatogo maja* has past time reference in this example, this is not part of the meaning of the adverbial (when used on the thirteenth of May, this adverbial would have future time reference). The rule restricting collocation refers crucially to the meaning, not the time reference, of expressions.

Let us now return to indirect speech in English. If we take a sentence like *John said that he would leave*, there are (at least) two ways in principle in which one could account for the future in the past in the subordinate clause. First, it might be the case that the verb is in this form because of its time interpretation relative to the present moment, i.e. the reporter's deictic centre would be the determinant. Secondly, it might be that English simply takes over into indirect speech the tense of the first speaker's original words, however superimposing on this a sequence of tense rule whereby after a main clause verb in the past tense the verb in the subordinate clause must be shifted back into the past relative to the tense used in direct speech; on this analysis, English would be like Russian except for the addition of the sequence of tenses rule. At the beginning of this section, we saw that other deictics in indirect speech in English require the first of these two analyses. We shall now argue, however, that for tense the second analysis is correct, i.e. the future in the past in the above example is determined not by the speaker's deictic centre, but rather by a syntactic rule which takes the tense of the original speaker's words (*I will leave*), and puts them into the corresponding past tense: here, the correspondent of the future is the future in the past. The analysis will be justified by showing examples where the first analysis fails to make correct predictions, or even makes incorrect predictions, whereas the second analysis makes correct predictions in all such cases, as well as in those cases where the first analysis by chance gets things right. The two analyses will be referred to as, respectively, the deictic centre analysis and the sequence of tenses analysis.

One piece of evidence separating the two analyses is indirect speech after a main verb in the future tense. Under the deictic centre analysis, a present tense in direct speech should appear as a future in such indirect speech; under the sequence of tenses analysis, the tense would remain unchanged, since the main verb is not a past tense. In fact, to report John's words *I am singing* in indirect speech one gets *John will say that he is singing*, and not *John will say that he will be singing*. The latter sentence is, of course, perfectly acceptable, but it differs in meaning from what is intended: it refers to a situation where John's singing is subsequent to the time of his utterance, i.e. where John's actual words are *I will be singing*. The acceptability of this second sentence shows that the exclusion of the future from *John will say that he is singing* has nothing to do with possible restrictions on the occurrence of the future tense in subordinate clauses in English (see section 5.4). Under the deictic centre analysis, the incorrect prediction would be made that both *I am singing* and *I will be singing* should have the same form in indirect speech after a main verb in the future tense, namely *John will say that he will be singing*.

Even more compelling is a second piece of evidence, which concerns the interpretation of past tenses in indirect speech after main verbs in the future (or more generally with future time reference). Let us return to a situation used above in the discussion of Russian. Imagine that today is the fifteenth of May. I make a prediction that John will utter the following words on the twentieth of May: *I arrived on the sixteenth of May*. The deictic centre and the sequence of tenses analyses make clearly different predictions here. Under the deictic centre analysis, since the sixteenth of May is in the future relative to the present moment, at which I am reporting John's words, the verb in the indirect speech should be in the future. Under the sequence of tenses analysis, since the tense in John's original words is past, and since there can be no shift in tense given that the main verb is non-past, the past tense of direct speech should be retained. Of course, the correct form is *John will say on the twentieth of May that he arrived on the sixteenth of May*, thus vindicating the sequence of tenses analysis. With this interpretation, it is quite impossible to say *John will say on the twentieth of May that he will arrive on the sixteenth of May*, since the tense of the indirect speech indicates that John's arrival will be subsequent to the time of his utterance, but this is contradicted by the time adverbials, given that the sixteenth of May comes before the twentieth of May (assuming that we are restricting ourselves to a single year).

Since, in the given example, *the sixteenth of May* and *tomorrow* are coreferential, we might try replacing the date by the time adverbial with the present moment as deictic centre (bearing in mind that this is the general principle for deictics other than tense in indirect speech). This would give the sentence *John will say on the twentieth of May that he arrived tomorrow*. For some speakers of English, this sentence is fully acceptable (at least once the interpretation is grasped). For other speakers, it is marginal or totally unacceptable.[9] Speakers who reject this sentence seem to have a constraint similar to the one discussed above for Russian, namely that it is impossible for them to collocate a tense which has a certain time reference meaning with an adverbial that has a time reference meaning incompatible with the meaning of that tense. Thus, in our example, *arrived* (past tense) has past time reference as part of its meaning, while *tomorrow* has future time reference as part of its meaning, and this violates the collocation restriction. The fact that *arrived* is actually assigned a future time reference interpretation is irrelevant. The version with *the sixteenth of May* is acceptable, since future time reference is not part of the meaning of the adverbial, only an interpretation that is assigned in this context. In English, incidentally, for speakers who reject *John will say that he arrived tomorrow*, the restriction is only against temporal uses of the past tense. The past tense in hypothetical conditionals, which have non-past time reference, is perfectly compatible with adverbials having future time reference as part of their meaning, e.g. *if John arrived tomorrow I'd be really happy*.

Another set of data where the deictic centre analysis makes an incorrect prediction but the sequence of tenses analysis makes the correct prediction concerns the tense of verbs in indirect speech that happen to have present time reference (from the viewpoint of the reporter), but are embedded under main verbs with past or future time reference. Let us suppose that John's actual words are *I will be absent on the fifteenth of May,* and that he said this about a week ago (and bearing in mind that we are imagining that today is the fifteenth of May). Under the deictic centre analysis, since today is the fifteenth of May, this should be reportable as *John said that he is absent on the fifteenth of May/today*, but in fact this is impossible with the intended interpretation. Similarly, if a week from now John says *I was absent on the fifteenth of May*, according to the deictic centre analysis this should be reportable as *John will say that he is absent on the fifteenth of May/today*. Again, this sentence is in fact impossible in the intended interpretation. According to the sequence of tenses analysis, the second of

---

[9] It may be that for at least some of these speakers the problem is rather one of constructing a plausible situation upon hearing a collocation that is apparently internally contradictory, rather than strictly a case of ungrammaticality. I am not sure at the moment how to distinguish empirically between these two possibilities.

these sentences will involve no change in the tense used in indirect speech, since the main verb is not a past tense, thus giving correctly *John will say that he was absent on the fifteenth of May/today*. (Note that the adverb *today* is compatible with all of present, past, and future tenses, since today encompasses not only the present moment but also a number of preceding and following time points.) For transposition into indirect speech of *John said, 'I will be absent on the fifteenth of May'*, the sequence of tenses analysis predicts that the future tense of the direct speech will be shifted to future in the past after the main verb in the past tense, giving *John said that he would be absent on the fifteenth of May/today*, correctly.

To conclude the discussion of data relating to the distinction between the deictic centre and sequence of tenses analyses of tense in indirect speech, we should also consider the example *John said that he would arrive (yesterday)*, as a report of John's actual words *I will arrive on the fourteenth of May*. The sequence of tenses analysis correctly predicts the future in the past here: the main verb is in a past tense, therefore John's actual words must be shifted into the past tense corresponding to the future, i.e. the future in the past. The occurrence of the future in the past is not incompatible with the deictic centre analysis, since, as was noted above, this example of indirect speech establishes a reference point in the past (John's saying) and then locates a situation in the future relative to that reference point. However, under the deictic centre analysis the past tense should also be possible, since John's arrival is located in the past relative to the present moment (recall that we are imagining that it is the fifteenth of May), so that with the same interpretation it should also be possible to say *John said that he arrived yesterday*. However, this sentence, while fully acceptable, does not have the same meaning as the sentence with the future in the past: in particular, it is compatible with a situation where John's arrival preceded his utterance, which is not possible when the future in the past is used. This thus gives a further piece of evidence in favour of the sequence of tenses analysis and against the deictic centre analysis. We therefore conclude that in English, the tense of direct speech is retained in indirect speech, subject to an added requirement that if the main verb is in a past tense, the tense of the original speech is shifted back into the past. The remainder of this section will be concerned with refinements of this statement.

The English sequence of tenses rule, like that discussed above for Spanish, is subject to one interesting modification. Even when the main verb is in a past tense it is possible (though not obligatory) to avoid invoking the shift to past sequence in the subordinate clause provided that the content of the indirect speech still has validity. Thus I can report John's

Indirect speech in English and Russian

actual words *I am ill*, spoken in the past, either as *John said that he was ill* or as *John said that he is ill*. In the former version, no commitment is made as to whether John's (actual or alleged) illness is a state continuing up to the present. In the second version, however, it is necessarily the case that I am reporting a (real or imaginary) illness which I believe still has relevance. One could use this version, for instance, if someone asked why John is not at work today, in which case the question makes clear that whatever answer is given must have current validity. The same failure to apply of the sequence of tenses rule can be seen with other tenses in the subordinate clause, e.g. *John said that he would/will leave tomorrow*; one cannot, of course, have **John said that he will leave yesterday*, where the time reference of the subordinate clause clearly has past time reference, not continuing validity. A more complex example is reporting *I will leave before Jane returns*, as said by John in the past. It is possible to leave both subordinate verbs in the non-past, i.e. *John said that he will leave before Jane returns*, with the implication that John's leaving and Jane's return are possible future events. It is also possible to leave just the last verb in the non-past, i.e. *John said that he would leave before Jane returns*, which leaves open the possibility that John has already left, but implies that Jane has not yet returned – this version could naturally be followed by . . . *and he has/did*, which cannot be appended to *John said that he will leave before Jane returns*. The version with both verbs shifted to past sequence, i.e. *John said that he would leave before Jane returned*, is the only version possible if John has in fact already left and Jane has already returned – this version could be followed by . . . *and he has/did.*[10]

The fact that one can retain non-past tenses in sentences like *John said that he is ill*, where the content of the reported speech has continuing validity, might seem to be an argument in favour of the deictic centre approach to tense in indirect speech in English: given that the illness is reported as holding at the present moment, the present tense is the obvious tense to use. However, adoption of the deictic centre analysis, quite apart from all the wrong predictions already discussed, does not account for the range of data found here, in particular since it is still possible to use the past tense (i.e. *John said that he was ill*) even if John's illness still has present

---

[10] It is not possible to leave just the first verb in the non-past, i.e. **John said that he will leave before Jane returned*. If the option of leaving a given verb in the non-past is exercised, then this option must be extended to all subordinate verbs. The relative time reference of the verbs is irrelevant, cf. *John said that he would/*will leave after Jane returned, John said that he would/*will sing while I was here*. The versions with asterisks become acceptable if the final clause verbs also remain in the non-past, i.e. replacing *returned* by *returns* and *was* by *am*.

time validity (although, of course, in this case the present validity is not made explicit). It is therefore preferable to maintain the sequence of tenses analysis, supplemented by the relaxation for verbs that have continuing validity, in precisely the same way as was done in section 5.2 for the subjunctive in Spanish.

The fact that English has a sequence of tenses rule leads to an interesting observation concerning the sentence *John said that he would arrive yesterday*, where the temporal reference of the subordinate verb is future relative to a reference point in the past, established by John's utterance, and also past with reference to the present moment. In this sense, the sentence is a mirror-image to *John will say that he arrived tomorrow*, where the temporal reference of the subordinate verb is past relative to a reference point in the future, established by John's utterance, and also future with reference to the present moment. Above, we noted that the second sentence is unacceptable for some speakers of English. Such speakers do not, however, have any similar problems with the first sentence. In Russian, literal translations of both sentences are unacceptable. Above, we accounted for these unacceptability judgements in terms of a restriction against collocating tenses and adverbials whose meanings conflict in time reference. Crucially, while this constraint rules out both Russian sentences and the second English sentence discussed in this paragraph, it does not exclude the first English sentence with the future in the past in the subordinate clause. Although the English future in the past does not necessarily have (absolute) past time reference, its meaning (future relative to a reference point in the past) is not incompatible with past time reference, i.e. there is no conflict between the meaning of the future in the past and the meaning of a past time adverbial like *yesterday*. We thus predict that this sentence should be acceptable even for speakers of English who have the constraint against collocating tenses and adverbials with conflicting time reference meanings. This correct prediction is further evidence in favour of the various claims made in this chapter, as here they interact in a particularly intricate way.

In stating the sequence of tenses rule, we noted that a verb in a non-past tense must be replaced by the corresponding past tense when the main verb is a past tense (subject to the option of not doing so when the situation referred to by the subordinate verb has continuing validity). What happens, however, if the verb in direct speech is already in the past tense? Here, English allows two possibilities. Thus, if one wants to report *John said, 'I arrived on Friday'* in indirect speech, either one can replace the simple past by the pluperfect to give *John said that he had arrived on Friday*, or one can simply leave the verb in the simple past *John said that he arrived on*

Friday.[11] This suggests that there are in fact two slightly different versions of the sequence of tenses rule, either of which may be applied. In the first variant, a tense in direct speech must be put into the corresponding past tense, so that a past tense in direct speech simply remains in the past, given that the past corresponds to itself across the non-past/past dichotomy. In the second variant, a tense in direct speech must be put into the past tense expressing one added degree of anteriority. For most tenses in direct speech, the two rules have the same effect, but for a past tense in direct speech they produce, respectively, the simple past and the pluperfect. In fact, the second variant must be supplemented by a restriction 'provided such a tense exists'. Thus, if the pluperfect occurs already in direct speech, it simply remains in indirect speech, as in reporting *I had seen her before yesterday* as *John said that he had seen her before yesterday*, since English does not have any tense that would express anteriority to the pluperfect (***. . . *that he had had seen . . .*).[12]

In this section, we have attempted to show how the interaction of a small number of simple principles leads naturally to the intricate and at times seemingly contradictory behaviour of tenses in indirect speech in English. Crucially, one of the principles involved is the meanings assigned to the various tenses, meanings that remain constant, but interact with and are crucially referred to by other principles to give time reference interpretations which at first sight seem to contradict the meanings of those tenses.

5.4 Future time reference in English subordinate clauses

In this section, we shall examine one very specific set of data from English, as an illustration of the complexity of interaction that can obtain between meanings of tenses and other aspects of the syntax of a language.[13] As already discussed, in general English requires overt grammatical representation of future time reference, for instance by means of the future tense, or close paraphrases (such as *going to*). Thus, in English one

---

[11] The two versions seem to be distinguished stylistically, the version with the pluperfect being more literary, the version with the simple past more colloquial.

[12] In fairness, it should be noted that the alternation of pluperfect and simple past here could be treated as an argument in favour of the deictic centre analysis of tense in indirect speech in English, and against the sequence of tenses approach: the past tense would be justified here since the time reference is indeed prior to the present moment, the pluperfect since the time reference is prior to the reference point established by the time reference of the main verb in the past. However, given that the deictic centre analysis makes so many incorrect predictions, it is preferable to continue to maintain the sequence of tenses analysis, albeit with a slight wrinkle to account for the alternation of pluperfect and simple past.

[13] The discussion of this section is essentially a condensation of the material presented in Comrie (1982), which also includes some comparison with other languages.

can say *it will rain tomorrow* or *it's going to rain tomorrow* but not, under normal interpretations, *it rains tomorrow*, even though the time adverbial makes the future time reference clear lexically. Only where reference is to a scheduled event can the present be used with future time reference, as in *the train leaves tomorrow morning at seven o'clock*. This generalisation holds for main clauses and some subordinate clauses. In a wide range of subordinate clauses, however, we find that the future tense is either impossible, being replaced by the present with future time reference even in the absence of scheduling, or exists only as an alternative to the present tense, as in the following examples:[14]

> *If you go/*will go out in the rain, you'll get wet.*
> *When you go/*will go out in the rain, you'll get wet.*
> *And then you'll come to an eagle which is/will be killing a snake.*

In what follows, we shall concentrate on conditional clauses, as these provide the most interesting interplay of factors, especially in so far as they permit a wide range of temporal relations between the situations referred to in the two clauses.

First, it should be noted that the restriction applies to the future tense, i.e. the form using the auxiliary *will/shall*. Other expressions of future time reference are not affected, in particular the *going to* periphrasis, so that one can say *if you're going to go out in the rain, you'll get wet*. We may therefore formulate a preliminary rule according to which in certain subordinate clauses, in particular conditional and temporal clauses, the future tense is replaced by the present tense. This rule overrides the meanings of the forms, so that even though *you go out in the rain* cannot be assigned future time reference (in the absence of scheduling), this time reference is possible for the present tense in the appropriate subordinate clauses. We thus have a further instance where a syntactic rule accounts for an apparently anomalous use of a tense, relative to the time reference meaning of that tense.

In fact, it turns out that the precise nature of this rule is more complex, as can be seen if we consider the time relation between the situation referred to in the subordinate clause and the situation referred to in the main clause. In our first example, i.e. *if you go out in the rain you'll get wet*, the time reference of the subordinate clause is anterior to that of the main clause.

---

[14] Some of the asterisked sentences here and below have other interpretations, irrelevant to the issue at hand, for instance modal rather than temporal interpretations of *will*. Some of the conditional clause examples also have possible interpretations involving more complex temporal and other relations, as discussed below and in Comrie (1982).

One can construct similar examples where the time references of the two clauses are the same (or overlap), as in *if you're still here at six o'clock we'll talk then*, where the time reference of both clauses is *at six o'clock*. Suppose, however, that the time reference of the subordinate verb is subsequent to that of the main verb. Such situations are possible, though no doubt less frequent in actual language use, and all one needs to do is think up some situation where something that happens in the relatively close future can be made dependent on something, or at least the promise of something, that will happen in the more distant future. Thus I may promise to give you some money in advance on condition that thereafter you do some shopping for me (say, with the inducement of your being able to keep the change). It is impossible to report this in English by using the present tense in the subordinate clause, i.e. *if you do the shopping for me I'll give you some money*, which can only be used (excluding habitual interpretation) to report a situation where the transfer of money is anterior to or simultaneous with the shopping expedition. To express the required time relation between the clauses, one can either use the *going to* periphrasis or the future tense, i.e. either *if you're going to do the shopping for me, I'll give you some money* or *if you'll do the shopping for me, I'll give you some money*. Since the rule restricting the future tense in subordinate clauses makes no reference to the *going to* periphrasis, there is no problem about its occurrence here – this periphrastic form is possible wherever its meaning is appropriate.[15]

This might suggest amending the earlier rule to say that replacement of the future tense by the present tense takes place where the verb in question has absolute future time reference and also non-future time reference relative to the verb of the main clause. This states correctly that where the temporal relation between the two clauses is subordinate before or simultaneous with main, then the present tense is possible and the future tense is impossible. When the time relation is subordinate after main, it correctly predicts that the present tense is impossible (unless, of course, it is permitted by other factors, in particular scheduling). However, it also predicts that under this last set of circumstances the future tense would always be possible. Unfortunately, this is not invariably the case. Imagine the following set of circumstances: I believe that at some time in the reasonably near future it is going to rain; I notice that you are about to go

---

[15] It follows from this that the *going to* construction expresses nothing about the relative temporal relation between main and subordinate clauses, but only an absolute time relation to the present moment. Thus the example sentence *if you're going to do the shopping for me I'll give you some money* is possible whether the addressee's doing the shopping is prior to, simultaneous with, or subsequent to the speaker's transfer of money to the addressee.

out; I feel that you should take your umbrella with you in order to avoid getting wet should it start raining. Then, with the *going to* construction, it is easy to construct a conditional clause with the required temporal relations between the two clauses and between each clause and the present moment: *if it's going to rain, you should take your umbrella*. However, even given this set of temporal relations, it is not possible to say **if it'll rain, you should take your umbrella*.

Thus under certain circumstances, in a conditional clause with future time reference, neither the present nor the future tense is possible. It is necessary to specify what those conditions are, in particular the conditions that permit *if you'll do the shopping for me I'll give you some money*, but not **if it'll rain you should take your umbrella*. The crucial difference is that in the first example there is a causal relation between my giving you some money and your doing the shopping: the sentence is acceptable only if this causal interpretation is assigned. In the second example, there is no such causal relation. Or rather, it is implausible that there should be a causal relation between your taking your umbrella and the subsequent occurrence of rain. In fact, if one accepts such a causal relation, i.e. if one believes that it is possible to make it rain by taking an umbrella, then the second sentence becomes perfectly acceptable. Thus what is crucial is a causal relation going from the main clause to the subordinate clause.

We can now summarise by formulating the rule for the occurrence of tenses (present tense and future tense, excluding the *going to* construction) in conditional clauses with future time reference. If the time reference of the subordinate clause is not subsequent to that of the main clause, then the present must be used in the conditional clause. If the time reference of the subordinate clause is subsequent to that of the main clause and there is a causal relation from the main clause to the subordinate clause, then the future tense must be used in the conditional clause. If the time reference of the subordinate clause is subsequent to that of the main clause and there is no such causal relation, then neither present nor future may be used in the conditional clause. The interaction of factors in this example is particularly complex, perhaps even surprising (e.g. as to why the causal relation between clauses should be relevant to tense use), but it is precisely this complexity which indicates how the interaction of various principles can lead to uses of tenses which at first sight go counter to their time reference meanings.

This chapter has attempted to add flesh to the claim that apparent exceptions to the meanings of tenses can often be accounted for in terms of the interaction with other factors, rather than simply abandoning a given proposed meaning for a tense as soon as an apparent counter-example is found. In some instances the principles that interact with the meanings of tenses are of great generality, such as the sequence of tenses rules found in many languages. In other instances, they may be very specific, such as the use of tenses in conditional clauses in English. An even more specific example in English concerns the use of the present tense of verbs of reporting, such as *say*, with past time reference, provided that the context of the report has continuing validity. Thus, in reporting John's past utterance *I am ill* it is, of course, possible to say *John said that he was ill* (or . . . *is ill*), but it is also possible to say *John says that he is ill*, even though his utterance is clearly in the past. The necessity for continuing validity can be seen in that one can say *John said that he was ill, but now claims to have recovered*, but not **John says that he is ill, but now claims to have recovered*. This is a very specific piece of information about a narrowly restricted range of lexical items in English, but still illustrates the general principle that apparent counter-examples to tense meanings can often be accounted for by interaction with other principles.

6
Conclusion: Towards a formal theory of tense

The aim of this chapter is to draw together the major claims set out in chapters 2–5, in particular showing how the generalisations established in those chapters should constrain any formal theory of tense. The aim of this chapter is thus not to build up such a formal theory, but rather to indicate what results of the cross-language study of tense should be taken into account by those who do wish to set up such a formal account.[1] The presentation follows overall the order of presentation of the earlier chapters.

6.1 **Absolute tense**

In order to establish formal representations of absolute tense, it is necessary to specify the present moment, which we shall henceforth abbreviate as S (for moment of speech). In addition, we need to specify a time point or interval which is occupied by the situation to be located in time; we shall refer to this time point or interval as E (for moment of event, though without restricting the use of this abbreviation specifically to events, rather than to situations in general). Notice that E is simply the time at which the situation is located, and is therefore neutral as to whether this is a point or an interval of time longer than a point. Finally, we need to establish some temporal relations that enable us to relate S and E to one another (more accurately, E to S, since we take S as given). The relations in question are *before*, *after*, and *simul(taneous)*. The relations *before* and *after* have essentially their ordinary-language meanings, i.e. on the time line an interval X is before an interval Y (*X before Y*) if and only if each time

---

[1] The representations are similar to those suggested by Reichenbach (1947), but with crucial modifications introduced by Comrie (1981); the latter article compares the two systems comprehensively. For absolute and absolute-relative tense, our representations turn out to be conceptually very close to those proposed by Jespersen (1924: 254–257), though with the addition of the possibility of multiple reference points. Bull (1963: 20–33) provides a schema that allows for two reference points, and thus can represent the temporal value of the English conditional perfect, but does not make the generalisation to an indefinite number of reference points.

point within X is to the left of each time point within Y; *X after Y* means that each time point within X is to the right of each time point in Y. The relation *simul* is defined as follows: *X simul Y* means that each time point in X is also in Y and vice versa. *Simul* is, of course, a symmetrical relation, i.e. *X simul Y* is equivalent to *Y simul X*. As far as tense as a grammatical category is concerned, finer distinctions within the *simul* relation are not required, i.e. languages do not have distinct grammatical categories of tense indicating location in time at a particular point versus location in time surrounding a particular point. The relations *before* and *after* are, of course, converses of one another, i.e. *X before Y* is equivalent to *Y after X*. Only one of them need therefore be specified as a primitive of the theory, though it seems to be arbitrary which one is chosen. It will become clearer in later sections why both relations are needed.

Given these two time points (*S, E*) and the three relations (*simul, before, after*), we can now represent the three absolute tenses present, past, and future, as follows:

present	*E simul S*
past	*E before S*
future	*E after S*

From a formal viewpoint, the decision to write *E* to the left of *S* is arbitrary, i.e. one could equally well write *S simul E, S after E,* and *S before E,* respectively, although the choice of one set of statements rather than the other should be made consistently; if the alternative formulation is chosen, it will be necessary to invert all other formulae in the same way. The order of presentation above does, however, have a certain intuitive appeal, since it locates *E*, the variable, in terms of the fixed point *S*, rather than vice versa.

Note, incidentally, that in order to incorporate a separate universal tense, it would be necessary to enlarge the theoretical apparatus, since our terms non-universal present and universal would both be represented as *E simul S*. If the claim of chapter 2 is correct, that natural languages do not distinguish universal tense, then this is a strong point in favour of the content of the representations suggested in this section: they permit representation of those distinctions that are made in natural languages, while disallowing representations of those distinctions of tense that are not made.

Before leaving absolute tense, it is necessary to consider the representations of tenses like non-past and non-future, especially given the widespread incidence of the former among the languages of the world. One solution would be to present a disjunctive definition:

non-past	*E simul S or E after S*
non-future	*E before S or E simul S*

However, such a disjunctive definition effectively denies the unity of representation of a single grammatical category, and should therefore be avoided in the absence of strong evidence in its favour. We therefore prefer to increase the theoretical apparatus slightly by allowing, in addition to the relations *before* and *after*, their negatives *not-before* and *not-after*, thus representing non-past and non-future as follows:

non-past	*E not-before S*
non-future	*E non-after S*

If the claim of chapter 2 is correct that no language has a non-present tense, then we should not define a relation *non-simul*, being the negative of *simul*.

In the representations just given, one might wonder why a relation of *not-before* (and likewise *not-after*) is developed, rather than just negating the representations for past and future to give, respectively: *not (E before S)*; *not (E after S)*. These representations, however, are crucially not equivalent to those suggested above as the correct representations. The correct representation for non-past, for instance, says that the situation is located within the time interval defined as *not-before S*, and this correctly locates the situation in this time interval, without saying anything about what situation may have held in the past (i.e. in the time interval defined as *before S*). The incorrect representations introduced for discussion in this paragraph, however, say only that the situation in question is not located before *S*, without saying anything about where it is located, or indeed whether it took place at all. Thus, *not (E before S)* is consistent with *E* being a non-existent situation, whereas *E not-before S* says explicitly that *E* is an actual situation, located temporally at some time within the time interval that is not before *S*, i.e. which includes *S* and all time points after *S*.

6.2 Relative tense

The representations in section 6.1 capture absolute tense distinctions by relating the situation (*E*) to the present moment (*S*). In order to capture distinctions of relative tense, all that is necessary is to establish a further time point, namely the reference point, symbolised *R*. We can then relate the location in time of the situation as simultaneous with, falling before, or falling after this reference point, as follows:

relative present	*E simul R*

relative past	*E before R*
relative future	*E after R*

Similarly, formulae can be derived mechanically for relative non-past and relative non-future from the parameters already discussed:

relative non-past	*E not-before R*
relative non-future	*E not-after R*

The major characteristic of all these representations for relative tense is that there is a reference point *R* which is not anchored, i.e. which is not itself located in time relative to any deictic centre, such as the present moment. This corresponds to the observation made in chapter 3 that the reference point for a relative tense is given by the context (and perhaps, by default in the absence of any other contextual indication, taken to be the present moment), but that the meaning of a relative tense does not contain any reference to the anchoring of the reference point.

6.3 **Combined absolute-relative tense**

Here we consider the representations for tenses like the English pluperfect and future perfect, in which, as discussed in section 3.2, a reference point is established relative to the present moment, and a situation is then located in time relative to that reference point. For the pluperfect, there is a reference point in the past (i.e. before the present moment), and the situation is located prior to that reference point, giving the representation:

pluperfect   *E before R before S*

This representation is to be interpreted as 'E before R and R before S'. A number of important properties of this representation should be noted. First, *E* is located relative to *R*, and *R* is located relative to *S*, but there is no direct relation established between *E* and *S*. Since the relation *before* is transitive (i.e. if X is before Y and Y is before Z, then necessarily X is before Z), one can deduce *E before S* from the representation of the pluperfect, but this is not part of the formal representation of the pluperfect; the import- ance of this observation will become clear when we discuss the future perfect. Secondly, the ordering of *E, R,* and *S* in the representation is such that *R* stands between *E* and *S*: this is true of all instances of combined absolute-relative tense, and corresponds to the intuition that with such combined tenses a situation is located relative to a reference point which in turn is located relative to the present moment.

Conclusion

The general structure of a tense representation within this framework can therefore be symbolised as *E (relative R) (relative S)*, where *relative* is a cover-symbol for all the permitted relations (*simul, before, after, not-before, not-after*). The formula covers the following special cases:

> *E*
> *E relative S*
> *E relative R*
> *E relative R relative S*

Other possibilities, such as a direct relation between *E* and *S* when there is also an *R* present, are not allowed by this system, which thus accords with the account given in the body of the book. Of the four schematic representations just given, *E relative S* corresponds to absolute tense, *E relative R* to relative tense, and *E relative R relative S* to combined absolute-relative tense. The representation *E* is allowed by the schema, but has not so far been discussed: it would, however, be appropriate for the representation of the temporal location of a situation in a language lacking tense altogether – such a situation is simply not located temporally by the grammatical system of the language in question.

Within this same system, the representation of the future perfect will be as follows:

> future perfect   *E before R after S*

The only difference between this and the pluperfect is that the reference point is in the future, rather than in the past, i.e. there is a sub-representation *R after S* corresponding to *R before S* in the pluperfect. Note once again that there is no direct relation established between *E* and *S*, and indeed all possible relations are compatible with the future perfect (i.e. *E before S, E simul S, E after S*); as was noted in section 3.2, the preference for interpretations where *E after S* holds is pragmatic, a conversational implicature, rather than part of the meaning of the future perfect. The representation given here has the great advantage that the future perfect does not turn out to be ambiguous, according to the relative temporal location of *E* and *S*, as is the case with Reichenbach's system.

The representation for the future perfect provides justification for a number of the characteristics of the kind of representation advocated in this chapter. First, it enables a relation to be established between *E* and *R* and between *R* and *S* without establishing a relation between *E* and *S*, and as was discussed in section 3.2 this is correct for the future perfect. In fact, the representation system advocated here would not permit a direct relation to be expressed between E and S where there is also an R present in the representation, and this correlates with the observation that no language distinguishes distinct 'future perfects' according to the relation between E and S. With the representation for the future perfect, unlike that for the pluperfect, it is not possible to deduce the temporal relation between E and S, since no relation between E and S can be deduced from the conjunction of E *before* R and R *after* S; this suggests the correctness of our representation of the pluperfect, where the fact that E *before* S is true is not part of the formal representation, but rather is derived by general logical principles given the transitivity of the relation *before*.

Secondly, the representation for the future perfect demonstrates that both of the relations *before* and *after* are needed in order to represent adequately the range of tenses found cross-linguistically. If one were just to use a single relation, say X—Y, meaning 'X is before Y', as is done by Reichenbach, then there would be no way of indicating E—R and S—R in a single representation without also establishing a relationship between E and S: and this is precisely the relationship that Reichenbach is forced to establish, with his three distinct representations for the future perfect: E—S—R; S—E—R; E, S—R (where the comma indicates simultaneity). The only possibility within Reichenbach's system avoiding this proliferation of representations would be a conjunctive formula of the type *(E—R) & (S—R)*, which effectively loses the concept of a unified representation for this grammatical category.

It is, of course, possible, as discussed in section 6.1, to invert all of the representations given in this chapter, replacing *before* by *after* and vice versa, i.e. there are equivalent representations:

pluperfect	S *after* R *after* E
future perfect	S *before* R *after* E

The inversion must, however, be carried out consistently, so that in the future perfect representation E *before* R *after* S it is not possible to invert only the first pair to give R *after* E . . . Consistent inversion simply means replacement of the abstract schema E *(relative R) (relative S)* by *(S relative) (R relative)* E.

One diagrammatic disadvantage of the representations suggested in this chapter is that left-right ordering, unlike in Reichenbach's system, does not mirror chronological order. In terms of capturing all and only the distinctions that are relevant cross-linguistically to tense systems, however, the present suggestion is clearly superior. It is possible to develop a visually more direct system, combining Reichenbach's notation with that used here, such that simultaneous situations are represented as separated by commas, and the dash is used to indicate chronological precedence (earlier situations stand to the left of the dash), while time points not linked by either a comma or a dash are unspecified as to their relative chronological order. In this system the representation for the future perfect would be as follows:

future perfect

While this representation is perhaps more direct visually, it is formally equivalent to the notations in our system, not to those in Reichenbach's, as can be seen crucially in the fact that the representation is no longer one-dimensional, as for Reichenbach. There is also a visual disadvantage in that one must not read this diagram to mean that S and E are simultaneous, i.e. left-right ordering does not correspond in all cases literally to chronological order.

Using the same representation schema, it is now easy to give representations for the future in the future and the future in the past (conditional):

future in the future   *E after R after S*

future in the past   *E after R before S*

These representations are thus similar to those for the pluperfect and the future perfect, only replacing the first *before* by *after*. For the future in the future, it is possible to deduce *E after S* from the transitivity of *after*, but this is not part of the formal representation. With the future in the past, just as with the future perfect, it is not possible to deduce the chronological relation between E and S, and indeed all three of the following are compatible with the representation given: *E before S*; *E after S*; *E simul S*.

A minor extension of the formalisation enables one to represent even more complex instances of time location, as when a situation is located relative to a reference point which is in turn located relative to a reference point which is located relative to the present moment. Thus, temporal uses of the conditional perfect (i.e. the future perfect in the past) can be symbolised as follows:

future perfect in the past   *E before R_1 after R_2 before S*

We can incorporate the possibility of multiple reference points in our general schema by replacing *(relative R)* by *(relative R)^n*. The general formula is thus *E (relative R)^n (relative S)*. In principle, the use of multiple reference points provides an infinite number of possibilities, jumping from one reference point to another. Of course, few of these are grammaticalised in any language. However, it is equally true that there is rarely need for such more complex representations – it soon becomes extremely difficult to compute the time location of a situation that involves several reference points – so it may well be that the non-existence of such referentially complex tenses has to do with practical restrictions, rather than with restrictions that should be built into the formal system. The formal system does have the advantage that tenses that are more complex cognitively are also given more complex representations.

6.4 Degrees of remoteness

So far, our representations have made no mention of degrees of remoteness. In principle, all that needs to be introduced to permit such specifications is replacement of the undifferentiated relations *before* and *after* by relations where quantity is specified as well as quality, i.e. where magnitude can be assigned to *before* and *after*. This could be done, for instance, by indicating the temporal distance between the two time points alongside the relation, as follows:

yesterday past tense   *E before S one day*

Before making any more specific proposals, however, it would be necessary to establish the cross-linguistic constraints on grammaticalisation of degrees of remoteness, a research endeavour that has only just been initiated. For the moment, then, all that can be said is that it will be necessary to have the mechanism to specify the magnitude of the relations *before* and *after*; we use the abbreviation *magn* to indicate such a specification of magnitude.

6.5 Tense combinations

Finally, we may consider tenses like those discussed in section 2.6, which involve reference to situations holding at more than one point in time, e.g. the 'still' and the 'no longer' tenses in some Bantu languages. Since the references to the two times are distributed between presupposition and assertion, we propose provisionally representations of the following kind:

'still' tense	presupp: E_1 before S
	assert: E_1 *simul* S
'no longer' tense	presupp: E_1 *before* S
	assert: *not (E_1 simul S)*

Conclusion

(The indexing of E is simply to indicate that the same situation is referred to in both parts of the formula.)

6.6 **Conclusion**

The final conclusion to this chapter, and to this book, can be given as a very succinct formula:

tense $\quad\quad E \ (relative \ R)^n \ (relative \ S)$
$\quad\quad\quad\quad\quad\quad magn \quad\quad\quad magn$

REFERENCES

Anderson, Stephen, C. 1983. 'Tone and morpheme rules in Bamileke-Ngyemboon.' PhD dissertation, University of Southern California, Los Angeles.

Arnott, D. W. 1970. *The nominal and verbal systems of Fula.* Oxford: Clarendon Press.

Ashton, E. O. 1947. *Swahili grammar (including intonation).* 2nd ed. London: Longmans, Green & Co.

Ashton, E. O., E. M. K. Mulira, E. G. M. Ndawula & A. N. Tucker. 1951. *A Luganda grammar.* London: Longmans, Green & Co.

Austin, J. L. 1962. *How to do things with words.* Oxford: Clarendon Press.

Bani, Ephraim & Terry J. Klokeid. 1972. *Kala Lagau Langgus: the Western Torres Strait Language: a report to the Australian Institute of Aboriginal Studies, Canberra.*

Breen, J. G. 1976. 'Simple and compound verbs: conjugation by auxiliaries in Australian verbal systems: Yandruwandha.' In R. M. W. Dixon, ed., *Grammatical categories in Australian languages,* pp. 750–756. Linguistic Series, 22. Canberra: Australian Institute of Aboriginal Studies & New Jersey: Humanities Press.

Bull, W. E. 1963. *Time, tense, and the verb: a study in theoretical and applied linguistics, with particular attention to Spanish.* University of California Publications in Linguistics, 19. Berkeley: University of California Press.

Carroll, John B., ed. 1956. *Language, thought, and reality: selected writings of Benjamin Lee Whorf.* Cambridge, Mass.: M.I.T. Press.

Cole, Peter. 1982. *Imbabura Quechua.* Lingua Descriptive Studies, 5. Amsterdam: North-Holland.

Comrie, Bernard. 1976. *Aspect.* Cambridge Textbooks in Linguistics. Cambridge: Cambridge University Press.

Comrie, Bernard. 1981. 'On Reichenbach's approach to tense.' In Roberta A. Hendrick, Carrie S. Masek & Mary Frances Miller, eds., *Papers from the Seventeenth Regional Meeting, Chicago Linguistic Society,* pp. 24–30. Chicago: Chicago Linguistic Society.

Comrie, Bernard. 1982. 'Future time reference in the conditional protasis', *Australian Journal of Linguistics* 2, 143–152.

Dahl, Östen. 1984. 'Temporal distance: remoteness distinctions in tense-aspect systems.' In Brian Butterworth, Bernard Comrie & Östen Dahl, eds., *Explanations for language universals,* pp. 105–22. Berlin: Mouton.

Derbyshire, Desmond C. 1979. *Hixkaryana.* Lingua Descriptive Studies, 1. Amsterdam: North-Holland.

Dixon, R. M. W. 1972. *The Dyirbal language of north Queensland.* Cambridge Studies in Linguistics, 9. Cambridge: Cambridge University Press.

Dixon, R. M. W. 1977. *A grammar of Yidiny.* Cambridge Studies in Linguistics, 19. Cambridge: Cambridge University Press.

Enç, Mürvet. 1981. 'Tense without scope: an analysis of nouns as indexicals.' PhD dissertation, University of Wisconsin, Madison.

References

England, Nora C. 1983. *A grammar of Mam, a Mayan language.* Texas Linguistics Series. Austin: University of Texas Press.

Fairbanks, Gordon H. & Earl W. Stevick 1958. *Spoken East Armenian.* New York: American Council of Learned Societies. Reprinted Ithaca, N.Y., 1975: Spoken Language Services.

Fillmore, Charles J. 1975. *Santa Cruz Lectures on deixis, 1971.* Bloomington: Indiana University Linguistics Club.

Fleischman, Suzanne. 1982. *The future in thought and language.* Cambridge Studies in Linguistics, 36. Cambridge: Cambridge University Press.

Forsyth, J. 1970. *A grammar of aspect: usage and meaning in the Russian verb.* Studies in the Modern Russian Language, extra volume. Cambridge: Cambridge University Press.

Gildersleeve, B. L. & Gonzalez Lodge. 1895. *Gildersleeve's Latin grammar.* London: Macmillan & New York: St. Martin's Press.

Glasgow, Kathleen. 1964. 'Frame of reference for two Burera tenses.' In Richard Pittman & Harland Kerr, eds., *Papers on the languages of the Australian Aborigines,* p. 118. Occasional Papers in Aboriginal Studies, 3. Canberra: Australian Institute of Aboriginal Studies.

Grice, H. P. 1975. 'Logic and conversation.' In Peter Cole & Jerrold Morgan, eds., *Speech acts,* pp. 41–58. Syntax and Semantics, 3. New York: Academic Press.

Haiman, John. 1980. *Hua: a Papuan language of the Eastern Highlands of New Guinea.* Studies in Language Companion Series, 5. Amsterdam: John Benjamins.

Hale, Kenneth. 1973. 'Person marking in Walbiri.' In Stephen R. Anderson & Paul Kiparsky, eds., *A festschrift for Morris Halle,* pp. 308–344. New York: Holt, Rinehart, Winston.

Hopper, Paul J. 1982. 'Aspect between discourse and grammar: an introductory essay for the volume.' In Paul J. Hopper, ed., *Tense-aspect: between semantics and pragmatics,* pp. 3–18. Typological Studies in Language, 1. Amsterdam: John Benjamins.

Hornstein, Norbert. 1977. 'Towards a theory of tense', *Linguistic Inquiry* 8, 521–557.

Hyman, Larry M. 1980. 'Relative time reference in the Bamileke tense system', *Studies in African Linguistics* 11, 227–237.

Hymes, Dell. 1975. 'From space to time in tenses in Kiksht', *International Journal of American Linguistics* 41, 313–329.

Imbs, Paul. 1960. *L'emploi des temps verbaux en français moderne: essai de grammaire descriptive.* Bibliothèque Française et Romane publiée par le Centre de Philologie romane de la Faculté des Lettres de Strasbourg, série A: Manuels et Études Linguistiques, 1. Paris: Klincksieck.

Jakobson, R. 1957. 'Shifters, verbal categories and the Russian verb.' Repr. in *Selected Writings,* vol. 2, pp. 130–147. The Hague: Mouton.

Javanaud, P. 1979. *Tense, mood, and aspect (mainly aspect) in Limouzi.* Gothenburg Papers in Theoretical Linguistics 39. Gothenburg: Department of Linguistics, University of Gothenburg.

Jespersen, Otto. 1924. *The philosophy of grammar.* London: Allen & Unwin.

Joos, M. 1964. *The English verb: form and meanings.* Madison & Milwaukee: University of Wisconsin Press.

Kellogg, Rev. S. H. 1893. *A grammar of the Hindi language.* 2nd rev. ed. Reprinted New Delhi, 1972: Oriental Books Reprint Corporation.

Kiparsky, Paul. 1968. 'Tense and mood in Indo-European syntax', *Foundations of Language* 4, 30–57.

Lancelot, C. & A. Arnauld 1660. *Grammaire générale et raisonnée.* Paris: Pierre le Petit.

Leech, Geoffrey N. 1971. *Meaning and the English verb.* London: Longman.

Longacre, Robert E. 1972. *Hierarchy and universality of discourse constituents in New Guinea languages: discussion.* Washington D.C.: Georgetown University Press.

Lyons, John. 1977. *Semantics.* Cambridge: Cambridge University Press.

McCawley, James D. 1981. *Everything that linguists have always wanted to know about logic but were ashamed to ask.* Chicago: University of Chicago Press & Oxford: Basil Blackwell.

McCoard, R. W. 1978. *The English perfect: tense-choice and pragmatic inferences.* North-Holland Linguistics Series, 38. Amsterdam: North-Holland.

Malotki, Ekkehart. 1983. *Hopi time.* Trends in Linguistics, Studies and Monographs, 20. Berlin: Mouton.

Marchese, Lynell. 1984. 'Tense innovation in the Kru language family', *Studies in African Linguistics* 15.

Morolong, M. 1978. 'Tense and aspect in Sesotho.' PhD dissertation, Simon Fraser University, Burnaby, British Columbia.

Okell, John. 1969. *A reference grammar of colloquial Burmese.* 2 vols. London: Oxford University Press.

Osborne, C. R. 1974. *The Tiwi language.* Australian Aboriginal Studies, 55. Canberra: Australian Institute of Aboriginal Studies.

Pitman, Donald. 1980. *Bosquejo de la gramática Araona.* Riberalta (Bolivia): Instituto Lingüístico de Verano & Ministerio de Educación y Cultura.

Randriamasimanana, Charles. 1981. 'A study of the causative constructions of Malagasy.' PhD dissertation, University of Southern California, Los Angeles.

Reichenbach, Hans. 1947. *Elements of symbolic logic.* New York: The Free Press & London: Collier-Macmillan.

Sapir, Edward. 1921. *Language: an introduction to the study of speech.* New York: Harcourt, Brace & World.

Schabert, Peter. 1976. *Laut- und Formenlehre des Maltesischen anhand zweier Mundarten.* Erlanger Studien, 16. Erlangen: Palm & Enke.

Searle, John R. 1969. *Speech acts: an essay in the philosophy of language.* Cambridge: Cambridge University Press.

Tereščenko, N. M. 1965. *Nenecko-russkij slovar', s priloženiem kratkogo grammatičeskogo očerka neneckogo jazyka.* Moscow: 'Sovetskaja ènciklopedija'.

Traugott, Elizabeth Closs. 1978. 'On the expression of spatio-temporal relations in language.' In Joseph H. Greenberg, Charles A. Ferguson & Edith A. Moravcsik, eds., *Universals of human language*, vol. 3: *Word structure*, pp. 369–400. Stanford: Stanford University Press.

Vannebo, Kjell Ivar. 1979. *Tempus og tidsreferanse: tidsdeiksis i norsk.* Oslo: Novus.

Whiteley, W. H. & M. G. Muli. 1962. *Practical introduction to Kamba.* London: Oxford University Press.

Woisetschlaeger, Erich F. 1977. *A semantic theory of the English auxiliary system.* Bloomington: Indiana University Linguistics Club.

Wright, W. 1898. *A grammar of the Arabic language*, vol. 2. 3rd ed., rev. by W. R. Smith & M. J. de Goeje. Cambridge: Cambridge University Press.

Wunderlich, Dieter. 1970. *Tempus und Zeitreferenz im Deutschen.* Linguistische Reihe, 5. Munich: Hueber.

INDEX OF LANGUAGES

For each language, I have specified its genetic classification in terms of genetic groupings of increasing size (separated by commas) and, after the semi-colon, its geographic location.

INDEX OF NAMES

INDEX OF SUBJECTS

Made in the USA
San Bernardino, CA
06 March 2013